HEALTH CARE

IN

VICTORIAN

EASTBOURNE

Warwick P Davis

2023

ISBN 978-0-9926161-5-1

9 780992 616151 >

CONTENTS

Acknowledgements.. i

List of Illustrations...ii

Chapters...iii

ACKNOWLEDGEMENTS

Content for the book has been collected from:

Newspapers of the time:

     Eastbourne Chronicle

     Eastbourne Gazette

     Eastbourne Herald

Eastbourne town directories:

     Gowland's Directory

     Pike's Directory

Eastbourne Local History Society

ILLUSTRATIONS

Illustration 1: Hellingly Asylum.....................................19

Illustrations 2/3: Ocklynge Cemetery.........................27

Illustration 4: Nursing Home advertisement..................64

Illustration 5: Homeopathic Convalescence Home..............67

Illustration 6: All Saints Convalescence Home....................72

Illustration 7: Dentists advertisement........................91

Illustration 8/9/10: Drinking Fountain 103

Illustration 11: Leaf Homeopathic Hospital......................124

Illustration 12: Princess Alice Memorial Hospital............... 132

Illustration 13: Sanatorium.....................................137

Illustration 14: Nurses advertisement............................. 202

Illustration 15: Nurses advertisement............................202

Illustration 16: Opticians advertisement...........................207

Illustration 17: Pharmacists advertisement.......................216

Illustration 18: Surgical Aid Society terms.......................226

Chapters

Introduction.. 1

Eastbourne Health - Ambulance..................................6

Eastbourne Health - Asylum.................................... 11

Eastbourne Health – Bunions and Corns.............................20

Eastbourne Health – Burial Board..............................23

Eastbourne Health – Common illnesses............................28

           Cancer..............................28

           Consumption...................................32

           Corpulency....................................37

           Diabetes.................................40

           Epilepsy................................43

           Hay Fever................................46

           Hysteria................................47

           Pneumonia................................49

           Scrofula................................51

Eastbourne Health – Constipation.........................55

Eastbourne Health – Convalescent and Nursing Homes...59

        Homeopathic Convalescent Home.........64

        All Saints Convalescent Home................68

Eastbourne Health – Cures and Quacks.................73

Eastbourne Health - Deafness.................82

Eastbourne Health - Dentists.................86

Eastbourne Health - Doctors.................92

Eastbourne Health – Drinking Water.................99

Eastbourne Health – Hazards.................104

   Arsenic.................105

   Mercury.................109

   Opium.................110

   Phosphorus.................112

Eastbourne Health - Hospitals.................115

   Acacia Villa.................115

   Iron Hospital.................116

   Leaf Homeopathic Cottage Hospital.117

   Princess Alice Memorial Hospital....124

   Sanatorium.................132

   Small Pox Hospital.................137

   St Luke's Children's Hospital.................142

   Union Workhouse Infirmary.................145

   Furniture Hospital.................150

Eastbourne Health - Hygiene.................151

Eastbourne Health - Hypnotism.................157

Eastbourne Health – Infectious Diseases.................163

   Cholera.................164

Diphtheria..168

Measles...173

Scarlet Fever.......................................175

Small Pox...179

Typhoid..184

Whooping Cough.................................188

Eastbourne Health – Nurses and Midwives.........................191

Eastbourne Health - Opticians.................................203

Eastbourne Health – Pharmacies and Dispensaries...........208

Eastbourne Health - Surgery...................................217

Eastbourne Health – Surgical Health Society.....................224

Eastbourne Health – Introduction

With a twenty first century health care system at our disposal it is difficult to imagine what a mid to late nineteenth century heath care system looked like but imagine 'healthcare' with:

- No hospitals
- No significant surgery
- Little or no anaesthetics
- Little or no disinfection, antisepsis, sterilisation
- No understanding of microbiology or infection
- No antibiotics or any medication of any effectiveness
- No aspirin, paracetamol, Calpol, steroids
- No chemotherapy, radiotherapy
- No trained nurses or midwives
- No technology: X rays, CT scans, MRI scans
- No diagnostic testing
- No blood transfusions, dialysis
- No organ transplantation
- No life support machines
- No Intensive, coronary care, special care baby units
- No 'free at the point of use' scheme
- Untried, untested medicines with dubious ingredients
- Over the counter access to poisons such as arsenic or drugs such as opium
- Expensive doctors with only a basic knowledge of anatomy and physiology
- Quackery on a large scale

- Rampaging and deadly infectious diseases
- Unsanitary, overcrowded living conditions

Such health care, if it could be described as such, that was available was ineffective, expensive and often out of the reach of the common person. Despite multiple medicinal concoctions being available through chemists and mail order they were universally unproven, ineffective, based largely on vegetable material with the occasional deadly components such as mercury or opium. Despite their ineffectiveness they were hailed in their marketing as miracle cures with the same medicine claiming to treat up to forty or fifty completely unrelated medical conditions often with guaranteed success.

The availability of health care services to the general population, or lack of them, was a major problem in the fight against disease and the restoration of health but some of the major impacts on the health of the general population were the living conditions especially in the rapidly growing manufacturing cities. The Industrial Revolution with the surge in manufacturing in factories throughout the country attracted huge numbers of families from the countryside with promises of regular and high pay. But the influx of workers and their families caused considerable difficulties with massive overcrowding in unsuitable and poorly constructed housing leading to many large families sharing a single house. The presence of outside privies, cess pits or general distribution of human waste impacted on the quality of the air which mixed with the pollution generated by the coal powered factories and homes severely degrading the atmospheric environment. But perhaps the most serious threat to health was the absence of any sanitation, drainage or sewer provision coupled with limited access to water that where available was often sourced from contaminated areas or from wells in close contact with poorly constructed cess pits or open sewers. Add in the poor nutrition that people could expect and there was a major recipe for disease to spread with little to combat it.

But not all towns and cities were the same. At the end of the eighteenth century the *European Magazine* described Eastbourne, with only a population of 2000 at the time, as "one of the favourable retreats for sickness, indolence and dissipation".

In 1833 the keen and ethereal air of this exalted spot (Eastbourne) would be seen almost capable, with the permission of the presiding and conservatory spirit of restoring vigour to the dying.

The town was often praised with five star reviews:

"When I came here, sir, I felt that I should be thankful if I could live a year but in fact, sir, I soon got a new inside and am now as well as I ever was."

"I never enjoyed good health in London, nor did my family, in fact we seldom had the doctor out of our house. Since I came here we have scarcely ever been ill. I never had better health and my son of twenty years is a strapping youth six feet high."

In 1883 after making a diagnosis a doctor prescribed a visitor from London a bottle of medicine with the remark that the splendid air of Eastbourne would do more good than any medicine. He said that such a testimony to the health of Eastbourne when the snow was on the ground spoke volumes in favour of the town as a winter health resort.

Fashionable crowds flocked year after year to enjoy the "salubrious climate and the eminently favourable hygienic conditions of the locality" (Eastbourne). Other watering places that were great and populous, whilst Eastbourne was in its infancy, now endeavoured to emulate its achievements.

Indeed the multiple benefits of Eastbourne not only enhanced its reputation as being a premier health resort but it also meant that the death rate of the inhabitants was consistently lower than other towns, especially on the south coast.

The position of the town beneath the Downs and alongside the sea benefitting from the clean air and bracing winds as well as the sound town planning providing wide, tree lined streets, good sanitation and drainage as well as clean water and the lack of heavy industry was at great contrast to the grim and unhealthy living conditions suffered by its neighbours in London.

Despite the lack of effective health care between 1850 and 1900 the life expectancy of an Eastbourne man rose from 40 to 45 years although workmen and labourers might have expected a shorter span. Over the same period the life expectancy for women increased from 42 to 50 years. Life expectancy for infants was considerably grimmer with an infant mortality rate in 1861 of 116 in 1000.

However there were exceptions and local folk were also keen to extol the virtues of Eastbourne. In 1894 at the annual general meeting of the Eastbourne Quoits club in the Lamb Hotel a local man, John Vine, gave a speech in which he was extremely enthusiastic over the hygienic attractions of the town. He said he was 82 years old and was born in Eastbourne. His father and grandfather were also natives. His grandfather had lived to the age of 99 and at 94 had never known what it was to have a head ache or tooth ache. He had brought up 23 children. The speaker had brought up 7 children himself the oldest now being 61 years of age none of them had had a medical attendant in their lives. He thought it spoke well of the health of Eastbourne.

Eastbourne was, at least in comparison, a healthy place to live but that did not mean it did not have its own health challenges. So what was available to the ordinary folk of the town when they were feeling a little under the weather?

Eastbourne Health – Ambulances

Today the concept of an ambulance service is firm in the minds of the population with, perhaps, three examples of the medical ambulance that people might bring to mind.

First there is the patient transport ambulance that takes patients to and from hospitals or clinics if they do not have access to or cannot afford private transport. Secondly there is the rather more glamorous air ambulance, usually in the form of a helicopter, which can land at the scene of major incidents delivering a highly skilled and experienced medical and para-medical team complete with advanced life saving/supporting equipment and medicines. High quality and often life saving care can be delivered at the site of any incident and then it can rapidly transport any patients to major trauma units in nearby hospitals. Thirdly there are the traditional ambulances which are high-tech mini hospitals staffed with highly qualified para-medical staff with a range of sophisticated life support and monitoring equipment that can stabilise and sustain a patient prior to and during their transportation to the nearest hospital under blue flashing lights and sirens.

The key to the definition of an ambulance, taken from the Greek for walking, in all three cases is the transfer of a patient from one place to a place where treatment could be administered. In the early to mid-nineteenth century the ambulance or more accurately a horse and cart was used, primarily, on the battle field. Casualties on the front line of a conflict were initially carried from the front line and transported in a simple horse drawn two or four wheeled cart adapted to carry a stretcher to areas where they could be treated. However in 1867 it was said in England that when the Crimea war began the pattern of construction of an ambulance had been lost and no-one in the country knew how to make one. The definition of the word ambulance was also confused when the term instead of it referring to a vehicle to transport casualties it was used for what we now recognise as a forward dressing station rather than a vehicle. In 1866 it was observed that the Prussian army used moveable ambulances that contained 22,000 beds, quite a large cart. As the soldiers were treated there they could then be transferred back from the line to the stationary hospitals containing 6,000 beds.

So the modern concept of ambulance transport is a vehicle that can take the case of illness or injury to the nearest hospital, probably to an accident and emergency or trauma centre. However, before 1883 when the Princess Alice Memorial Hospital was opened in Eastbourne there was no hospital to which patients could be taken and certainly no accident department so the ambulance of the time had a very different role. There were many reports in the local newspapers of the use of the police administered ambulance, there was no dedicated ambulance service as we know it today, in Eastbourne transporting bodies from their place of discovery to the mortuary or, quite often, to the police station in Latimer Road. It was acting more like a hearse or police vehicle, Black Maria, than an ambulance. When it was not transporting bodies though it was also used, controversially, to transport the town's

Medical Officer. In 1892 the Sanitary Committee discussed the fact that the medical officer was using the ambulance to convey himself to parts of the town, including Norway, and to attend the police incidents when requested. Although he claimed he needed transport to attend his calls across the ever growing town one committee member suggested he should use his legs rather than the ambulance and save the town an expense.

In 1894 a councillor called attention to a bill for £25 3s 0d for cab hire for the medical officer saying he thought once they had an ambulance horse they would save a great deal. It would appear the medical officer could not win. The councillor thought they had a horse to haul the ambulance but an alderman suggested they needed more than one. Of course they were not always successful in something as apparently simple as purchasing a horse. In 1892 the Sanitary Committee had issues about who gave the Borough Surveyor permission to spend £42 on a horse for ambulance work. A councillor asked who gave the instruction because he said he saw very few gentlemen in the meeting that knew the difference between a horse and a donkey. This must have been slightly odd as the whole of the country was totally reliant on horse power to move and there must have been a considerable body of equine knowledge in the town.

This lack of knowledge might have been well illustrated in 1892 when it was suggested the "poor, miserable Eastbourne rate payer" would not be amused that the Sanitary Committee had come into possession of a horse, albeit free of charge, which was addicted to jibbing. Jibbing being the habit of stopping and refusing to go forward. The horse in question which was left over as part of the deal to build the Sanatorium did indeed prefer to go backwards instead of forwards and when it was put in harness with the ambulance cart it would not, at first, move at all but then after a great deal of persuasion it decided to move backwards at a rate scattering the onlookers. Eventually it was noted the heroic Borough Surveyor leapt on to the ambulance driver's seat guiding the out of control horse to a gate where it stopped. The horse, being declared unsuited to ambulance work, was sold at auction and became a bus horse. The 'corporation jibber' as it came to be known died in 1894 in its stables in Old Town but not before it appeared on stage, or at least a Mr Jinman appeared on stage dressed as the jibber. It also became a standing joke at public dinners.

The costs of providing the ambulance service were always a concern. In 1877 the attention of the Eastbourne Board of Guardians was drawn to a highly desirable ambulance carriage but the board decided it already had one and did not need another. How much it was used was not known but in 1889 the Finance and Purchasing Committee reported they had considered the purchase of a wagon but the services of one had only been required once recently and, if the one and only patient who had used it had been removed to the hospital in time, it would not have been needed at all. Obviously a very inconsiderate patient who perhaps had had to wait too long for the ambulance to arrive so made their own way to assistance. Eventually one was purchased for the sum of £105 although in

1893 there was concern that the Sanitary Committee had not allowed sufficiently for the depreciation in regard to the ambulance and horse. In 1897 the annual cost of the police ambulance was said to be £15.

When not transporting citizens to the mortuary or police station or the Medical officer it was seen to be present at public events. In 1894 an ambulance was positioned in Gore Field, East Dean to take part in a war game exercise. In 1899 the police ambulance was on duty on both days of the Sussex Agricultural Society show in Eastbourne so that any casualty could be dealt with promptly. The ambulance was a common sight at public events and in 1902 had a new treatment in its armoury. At the Coronation celebrations the St John's Ambulance Association provided ambulance posts at every nook and corner resourced with ambulance, stretchers, bandages, splints and supplies of Oxo meat beverage.

The presence of the ambulance was becoming appreciated in the town and in 1902 calls were made to provide an ambulance station in Old Town and one to be kept in the fire station in Meads ready for any accidents at Beachy Head. But things did not necessarily move quickly in Eastbourne and in 1905 the calls were still not acted upon.

Eastbourne Health – Asylum

The current definitions of the word 'asylum' are "protection from danger" or "an institution for people who are mentally ill". It is derived from the Greek word 'refuge' and in the Victorian era perhaps 'refuge' was the more appropriate term.

It did mean a place of safety for people fleeing political turmoil or war and it was not always applied. In 1863 the Austrian government was condemned for not having the courage to afford asylum for the patriotic Poles seeking refuge for the brutal savagery of the Russian Cossacks.

It also meant an institution for people who were mentally ill although the definition of 'mentally ill' was very wide as was the terminology that called people lunatics, idiots, imbeciles or the insane or criminally insane. It also meant a place where people who were too fond of alcohol could be sent or a place where people with epilepsy could be kept.

But the word 'asylum' was also used for places where vulnerable or disadvantaged people could be looked after, trained to work, kept safe and supported. A list of legacies left in wills to various establishments and institutions illustrated the wide range of support and care that came under the heading of an asylum. Examples in the 1860s were: the British Orphan Asylum, the Albert Orphan Asylum, the Asylum for Fatherless Children, the London Orphan Asylum, the Female Orphan Asylum, the Deaf and Dumb Asylum, the Indigent Blind Asylum, the Asylum for Soldier's Widows, the Magdalen Asylums (laundries run along work house lines) for 'fallen women' and the Destitute Sailors Asylum. There were also specialist asylums for people not necessarily considered to be lunatics or insane but rather considered to be idiots such as the Orphan Asylum for Idiots and the plain old Asylum for Idiots. The potential clientele then as now must have been quite enormous.

The fact that there were so many places where the less fortunate could be looked after was, perhaps, testament to the difficulty people had in looking after family or relatives when faced with even harder times than they were used to. On the other hand it was perhaps something of a negative comment on potential carers who were keen to offload their responsibilities onto another agency. Nevertheless the presence of such a range of asylums was also testament to the generosity and public spirit of people who ran the asylums and who, generally through charitable donations, supported them.

There were plainly a large number of asylums that catered for groups that were not mentally ill and just needed social support but aside for what might be better described as homes for the vulnerable there were also a large number of what the modern person might assume an asylum was. That was a rather bleak, intimidating and secure institution that people were placed in, very often, against their will and for indeterminate lengths of time, possibly for life, and for a very wide range of diagnoses many of which would not be considered mental illness today.

There appeared to be plenty of candidates for treatment in the more extreme traditional form of secure, prison like, asylums that a current person might envisage. In 1867 the English Lunacy Commission reported there were 49,082 recognised lunatics in the country. In 1857 there were 33,791 meaning 1 person in every 570 of the English population was considered to be a lunatic. Of a total United Kingdom population of around 30,000,000 there were estimated to be 65,000 persons of unsound mind or 1 in 460 of the general population.

Assuming at one end of the 'lunatic' scale there were those diagnosed as being criminally insane. In 1865, at that extreme, there were around 500 inmates, 400 male and 50 to 60 female, at the Criminal Lunatic Asylum, known as Broadmoor nearly all of them homicides. It was perhaps slightly concerning they did not seem to know exactly how many inmates they had in the establishment. At the other end of the scale perhaps where the term 'lunatic' was very inaccurate was the Earlswood Asylum for Idiots in Redhill which, in 1892, had 620 severely afflicted patients requiring special care and education. They were especially appealing for funds to pay the bills. Other 'asylums' like the Infant Orphan Asylum in Wanstead in 1886 took in children under 7 and up to 15 years of age. The Royal Albert Orphan Asylum in Bagshot, Surrey held 220 destitute boys and girls and maintained them through child hood teaching them trades to support themselves when they left.

The 'local' traditional asylum was the Sussex County Lunatic Asylum was in Haywards Heath and was built in 1859. In 1888 it had 370 male and 478 female inmates, a total of 848 souls. At the time this was considered to be nearly full and the potential overcrowding required the removal of the old and chronic cases to the work houses to relieve congestion. In 1890 there were 823 inmates with 80 having to be sent to the Berrywood Asylum in Northampton. It appeared many towns had their own asylums as well as county institutions. The conditions in which inmates were kept was carefully monitored. In one inspection of the Haywards Heath asylum in 1889 it was declared all was well and that the diets the inmates enjoyed were the same as the visit in 1888 except that butter was now spread on the bread at breakfast. Obviously a significant improvement in the treatment of lunacy. Significantly 83 of the 'lunatic' inmates were identified as being epileptics. In 1893 the 'accumulation' of epileptics in asylums was being treated as a matter of great importance. It was noted that although their detention was a safe guard to the community at large there were many of them to whom an asylum was especially distasteful. Quite how or why the public needed safe guarding or why it was a surprise that epileptics did not want to be placed in a lunatic asylum is not explained. The fact that epilepsy was just a disorder of the electrical pathways in the brain completely escaped the asylum system which labelled them as part of the 'lunatic' population.

There were continual comments about the capacity of the asylum in Haywards Heath and frequent demands for a second institution. In 1889 it was suggested a second asylum could relieve the congestion by catering for imbeciles who could be monitored at half the cost charged for lunatics in asylums. Although in 1884 there were only 9 male and 10 females from Eastbourne in the county asylum none of them were considered fit for removal. The Sussex asylum management advised, in 1889, that should the need arise for more patients to be sent from Eastbourne patients could be sent directly to the Hants Asylum in Fareham although Eastbourne would be advised to check with Haywards Heath first because places were always becoming available. Alternatively patients could be sent to the asylum in Ipswich which currently had 60 vacancies for lunatics at 14/- a week.

Also to prevent any long distance transportation due to over-capacity the County Asylum asked the Eastbourne Guardians in 1876 not to send any lunatics with infectious diseases to them without prior notice and in 1879 to only send *bona fidae* paupers because if they did not a second asylum would certainly have to be built. The issue of capacity was, potentially, a problem as in 1874 an Eastbourne doctor was asked to investigate four cases at the County Asylum after it was claimed that people were being kept in unnecessarily so as to boost the numbers and lend weight to the argument for a second asylum. Of course no building could be big enough for the movement set up in 1867 proposing to house useless young men.

If the huge institutions were not to a patients liking there were private asylums like the Periteau which was a licenced private asylum in Winchelsea for five mentally afflicted ladies and it was conducted on the system of a private family with an utter absence of anything that could remind the invalids that they were under care. Of course not everything was quite so well ordered. In 1894 Dr Sherrard of Avalon House, Eastbourne was charged with unlawfully and without the consent and approval of the Commissioner of Lunacy receiving certain lunatics into his house with such house not being an institution for the reception of lunatics.

Many detailed and personal accounts of people being admitted to the asylums were reported in the newspapers with no consideration of patient confidentiality and, of course there were numbers who might well have benefitted from being in a well-regulated institution. But there were many cases where a lunatic asylum was the last place they should have found themselves. Epilepsy was a classic case where a medical condition was regarded as a mental one with risks and dangers to the general public. But epileptics were not the only inappropriate cases. In 1878 one unlucky bricklayer in Eastbourne was reported as being a wandering lunatic, sectioned and promptly sent to the county asylum but many others were sent there through the taking of strong drink. A Temperance Meeting in the Workmen's Hall in Eastbourne was told that nine out of ten of those in prison, union houses and lunatic asylums were there through strong drink. In 1882 a writer in the *Sunday Times* observed that a large percentage of inmates of the lunatic asylums were sent there through excess drink. So whatever the reasons whether it be so many people being sent to the asylums unnecessarily or the politics of keeping people in asylums just so the argument for more asylums could be made changes were afoot in Sussex.

In 1898 discussions were had with the Earl of Chichester for the purchase of 400 acres of Hellingly Park farm and part of Park Wood for £16,000 for the site of the new asylum. As always there were numerous discussions not least about the name for the new institution. Initially Amberstone was favourite but East Sussex Asylum was offered but eventually it was decided to call it Hellingly. In 1899 the Chairman of the Council announced that the new Lunatic asylum at Hellingly would cost £353,409. There were reservations about such a large building project and the ability to recruit builders. A new asylum in Newport, Isle of Wight was a frequent advertiser for winter or yearlong workers such as carpenters at $6\frac{3}{4}$ d an hour, bricklayers at $7\frac{1}{2}$ d an hour and good plasterers on good wages for a long job.

The proposed building would eventually hold 1,500 inmates. On hearing the costs it was claimed that Hellingly would cost five times the cost of the asylum being built in Brighton. To make matters worse the Clerk to the Visiting Committee of the Haywards Heath Asylum wrote stating that maintenance was ten shillings a week per patient but at Hellingly it was fourteen shillings a head for the luxury of living in that "palace". Hellingly was opened on July 20th 1903 and closed in 1994.

Humans were not the only species offered asylum. In 1867 an inspection was required of Miss Dear's Rottingdean Cat Asylum in 4 Ivy Cottage. The newspaper reporter visiting the site suggested he had never witnessed such a conglomeration of refined taste, misdirected kindness and abominable filth as he saw at the asylum. There were over a hundred dead, diseased and starving cats described as ugly, miserable looking creatures as well as dogs which were accused of actually causing the smell and not the cats, rabbits and birds all being kept in such squalid conditions that caused such a smell the neighbours had complained.

But even Eastbourne town itself could be described as an asylum perhaps meaning a place for escape rather than a place to be incarcerated. In 1871 there were complaints about a pernicious and foolish habit (now in vogue) of treating a seaside asylum such as Eastbourne as a pseudo-metropolis. It was suggested that if people wanted to show off then they should stay in town (London) and have their will. Eastbourne people were not the sort to "get up" extravagantly and if people wanted to do that then they should go to Brighton.

Should anyone say anything bad about Eastbourne it was suggested that they surely should be in an asylum just like the American medical man who wrote less than complimentary descriptions of lady cyclists who, if he was not already an inmate in a lunatic asylum was advised he could do well to visit Eastbourne in order to see some of our lady cyclists.

A complaint written in the Times newspaper in 1885 said that the summer season in Eastbourne was the resort of a large number of lunatics and that they cause great annoyance to the sane visitors who select Eastbourne as their seaside habitation. As a rebuttal it was suggested Eastbourne had only its proportion of imbeciles or lunatics.

Lunacy could be treated lightly though. In 1888 Edward Terry and the London Company produced a play called the Woman Hater by a Mr Lloyd at the Devonshire Park theatre. A character at one stage is mistaken for a lunatic and taken to a private asylum where, while no-one is insane everyone seems to think that everyone else is insane and there is a series of "excruciatingly funny scenes".

Even politics was not free from accusations of lunacy. In 1889 it was feared that the election excitement in Eastbourne over the County Council elections would result in additional lunatic accommodation being required.

Illustration 1: Hellingly Asylum entrance

Eastbourne Health – Bunions and Corns

If the description of the formation of a bunion in the 1880 edition of the *Family Physician* was representative it is a wonder anyone in Victorian Eastbourne managed to walk at all. The writer's conclusion was that bunions were due to ill-fitting boots. They described the toes as being screwed up together like bunch of carrots, the second and third toes sticking up over the others whilst the little toe was pushed under and quite out of sight with the big toe no longer in a straight line with the inner margins of the foot but forming a distinct angle with it.

Aside from the discomfort that must have ensued from such a crowded boot it was also important to look after one's feet as people were now having their fortunes told by having their feet read. Palmistry, which had swept through Eastbourne, was going out of fashion but if you needed to see the future or have your character determined it was possible to have a plaster cast taken of the right foot which was sent off to a professor of chiropody for analysis. By 1890 they had found that the broad soled, flat heeled feet showed a mean, grasping disposition, the high instep showed a nervous, passionate nature and the well-formed, neat little ankle illustrated self-consciousness and vanity.

Of course bunions and corns were painful and debilitating but help was at hand with numerous self-help cures. In 1882 Wilson's Corn Solvent was never known to fail and was a painless and rapid cure for bunions and warts. Holloway's ointments and pills were a definite cure-all in 1877 curing everything from bad breasts, piles, sore heads to bunions and corns.

If however you wanted some professional advice and treatment there was plenty on offer. In 1896 M Max of 57 Ashford Square was an experienced chiropodist who had moderate charges for his attendance at a patient's own home. In the same year Le Main and Challice skilfully and painlessly treated bunions, in-growing, nails and corns in 49 Terminus Road as well as manicures and face massages.

There were also international visits from renowned chiropodists. In 1871 Monsieur J Mayers, Practical and Experienced chiropodist from Paris, an Anatomical Professor of the Pathology of the Human Foot offered corn extraction for the instantaneous and effective cure of corns and bunions. He was to be found at 77 Terminus Road and claimed to be patronised by his Imperial Majesty Napoleon III. The eminent chiropractor Mr Siemms of Berlin and London announced in 1881 that he was intending to terminate his visit to Eastbourne and that all sufferers from corns, bunions, in growing nails or other affectations of the feet would do well not to delay paying him a visit at 116 Terminus Road. If you were concerned there was no cause to be as there was no question as to his skill. In 1881 Siemms charged five shillings for treatment for each corn with nails, bunions and warts being charged accordingly, He also offered half fees to servants and others from 6 until 8 every evening.

But there was also local talent. In 1882 Mr H Harriott described as being the energetic and obliging manager of the Devonshire Baths had, for some years, been studying chiropody and had operated with some success on the corns of several gentlemen in Eastbourne by painlessly extracting the same. He was now going to be allowed to practice at the Baths for anyone who desired to avail themselves of his services. He was available to ladies and gentlemen at the baths or they could be attended at their own residences.

He was obviously very successful as in 1884 he resigned as Devonshire Baths manager as he found the chiropody business so increased he could afford to separate himself from his duties as bath's manager. On leaving he was described as being a man of active intelligence, obliging manner and numerous individual merits. Blessed indeed was the fair foot which would get chiropodian relief from the skilful attentions of our respected townsman. Perhaps he could bring some order to the foot described by the *Family Physician*.

Eastbourne Health – Burial Board

The Metropolitan Burial Act was passed in 1852 and provided for the establishment of public cemeteries. Prior to this cemeteries, aside from the church yard, had been provided by private businesses and there were often complaints about the planning and layouts of their facilities. There were also concerns, particularly in times of large epidemic deaths of the potential for disease to escape the grave and infect the living. The need for more space for graves was a consideration for the parish church St Mary's whose burial ground was extended by the acquisition of "Pigeon House garden" but within ten years alternative sites were required.

In response to the Act in 1854 the Eastbourne Burial Board was formed being composed of nine ratepayers. Their role was to manage the cemeteries, fix the burial fees and ancillary charges and to sell the grave plots. In 1855 four acres of land known as Ocklynge Piece were purchased in Ocklynge for £2000 and were designated a cemetery. Initially there were complaints that the cost of provision was too great so the building of the planned entrance lodge was delayed to save money.

Over the history of the Ocklynge cemetery the Burial Board was often uncertain about the capacity and demand, possibly because of the 'healthiness' of Eastbourne and the relatively low death rate, and had to frequently purchase more land to expand the site but being careful not to buy too much. In 1873 the planned purchase of six acres was reduced to four acres and nine years later it was decided the plot would soon be full. Two and a half acres were consecrated ground and one and a half acres was as ground that was not consecrated but that was also to contain the porter's lodge and gardens. Ultimately the board gave up and purchased sixteen acres of land in Langney specifically to cater for the east end and the purchase was considered sufficient for the next 50 years. But this was significantly under used compared with the Ocklynge cemetery. In two months of 1887 there were 35 burials in Ocklynge but only 9 in Langney. The Ocklynge cemetery was predicted to be full in 50 years' time but it was considered that cremations would have been in full swing by then. In 1893 the Ocklynge cemetery was again enlarged north to Eldon Road.

Ocklynge cemetery was consecrated in April 1857 and one of the first to be buried there was Henry Ford (1781 – 1857). He was a builder originally from East Hoathly but was living in Fords House, 32 Seaside and reportedly one of the builders constructing the cemetery.

The Burial Board authorised the building of a lodge, dead house and "other necessary out offices" in 1862. The construction was obviously sympathetic and it was considered in 1884 that few towns possessed a cemetery so pleasantly sited as the Ocklynge cemetery pleasantly situated on the brow of a hill from which a magnificent view of the surrounding countryside was obtainable. However the entrance was considered very dismal and depressing with a high brick wall setting it out from the road. There were to be many discussions about the wall and calls for an ornamental wall and iron railings with trailing foliage to replace it.

It was reported that between 1878 and 1880 there had been 797 funerals with 142 burials in the ground that was not consecrated and 655 in consecrated. By 1881 to 1883 this had changed to 912 funerals with 212 in unconsecrated ground and 700 in consecrated. The new section in 1884 planned for an extra 1286 consecrated places and 460 unconsecrated and this was to be fenced off with poles and wire until a hedge grew in their place. Relief on the capacity demands for the cemetery did arrive as predicted with the Cremation Society being founded in 1874 and the first legal cremation in 1885.

There were, of course, problems. In 1886 the vicar of Eastbourne asked why pauper burials from the work house in Old Town took place in Langney instead of Ocklynge which was closer to hand. There were also claims of discrimination when in 1886 the Board of Guardians objected to the Burial Board fixing a higher scale of fees for Ocklynge than for Langney as the differential was making a distinction between the burial place for the rich, Ocklynge, and the one for the poor, Langney. It claimed the fees should be the same. The Board stated that the fee at Ocklynge was 7/6d and at Langney it was 5/- but this was due to a fee of 2/6d charged by the vicar at Ocklynge.

Grave diggers also complained they were being discriminated against with the ones at Langney being paid £1 a week with 3/- being paid in rent and this was not considered to be enough for this "unpleasant" work. It was pointed out that the Ocklynge diggers were paid the same and, somewhat provocatively it was said that they worked longer hours and presumably because of the greater activity they worked harder. Nevertheless in a burst of generosity the Burial Board asked if £1 a week was sufficient for a family man to survive. They concluded it was not and raised all the diggers' wages by two shillings a week.

Not everyone was so well pleased. In 1899 there were complaints about the daily and frequent tolling of the Ocklynge cemetery bell stating that it was causing serious results for local persons of a nervous temperament and those who may not have been in robust health. In addition there was the torture of the bell constantly reminding people of the end that awaited all. The writer of the complaint added that the dull and depressing weather being experienced rendered his petition all the more urgent. Discussions about the bell declared that it seemed pointless but, as was often the case in Eastbourne, a decision was postponed to a later date. For whom the bell tolls............

Illustration 2: Ocklynge cemetery from Willingdon Road

Illustration 3: Ocklynge cemetery from Eldon Road

Eastbourne Health – Common illnesses

Cancer

Cells that make up the human body are constantly dying and being replaced by new cells. The body, usually, regulates the production of these cells very tightly but occasionally the cells that are produced are abnormal and do not respond to the controlling mechanisms the body has or the methods of removing them. This means the cells proliferate out of control maybe as a solid tumour, for example a lung cancer or as a liquid tumour, for example leukaemia. The solid tumour may stay in one place or it may metastasise and spread to different parts of the body. Today there are over two hundred types of cancer identified but in the late nineteenth century, with the possible exception of stomach cancer, all cancers were considered to be the same and, of course aside from surgery, there was no treatment or cure for any of them.

There was, understandably an aversion to surgery to treat cancer or anything for that matter. In 1863 during an inquest on a man who had died of cancer it was noted that he had a tumour on his under lip which seemed like a cancer and it had spread to his throat causing him great pain. However he had steadfastly refused to consult a surgeon having decided, himself, that it was cancer and that there was no cure. On examination of the body the coroner found that the stomach contained prussic acid which was formed when cyanide came into contact with the cells of the gut. The conclusion was he committed suicide with an unsound mind.

To avoid such a fate in 1880 it was possible to get an abridged version of a book on cancer for five stamps offering the certainty of relief without operation. St Saviour's Cancer hospital in Osnaburgh Street, Regent's Park could also successfully treat cancers without the knife with terms of 30/- a week. There were specialist, charitable, cancer hospitals such as the Cancer hospital in Fulham Road, London surviving on legacies in wills such as the one in 1884 that left it and the Sussex County hospital in Brighton £1000 each. There was competition for legacies though as this one also left £3000 to the Asylum for Idiots in Redhill.

If you could not afford a week or more in treatment or five stamps then a 'Magnetic Physician' in America claimed to cure anything and everything by merely putting hands on any affected part. He could cure small pox in 15 minutes, stick broken bones like Spaulding's glue (a strong glue used for mending furniture, marble, shoes and billiard cues), stop haemorrhages (the bigger the blood loss the better the cure), cure all kinds of diseases including internal cancers and tumours although it was noted that internal cancers were easier to cure than external ones (possibly because no-one could see them?) and he could cure a stomach cancer with his hands alone.

America was obviously blessed with these practitioners because on 1887 a Dr J R Newton cured, with one treatment, a lady who had suffered with eye cancer for 15 years and another with a tumour as large as a person's head (site unspecified).

But surgery with all its risks might work. In 1883 it was reported that a surgeon in Vienna had removed a third of a patient's stomach and – strange to say - the patient recovered which says a lot about the success rate of surgery. It was claimed to be the only successful operation of the kind ever performed. The article did not say how many unsuccessful operations had been performed. The article went on to reassure people that 999 times out of 1000 the symptoms that might be of cancer were of dyspepsia and the best remedy for that was Seigel's Curative Syrup. A vegetable preparation that struck at the very foundation of the disease driving it root and branch out of the system.

In competition with the syrup in 1877 there was the world famous Blood Mixture for spots, pimples, pustules, boils and cancerous ulcers. Or in 1889 Frazer's Sulphur tablets were a gentle laxative because the harsh purgative pills that were used for constipation would cause it to become chronic destroying the mucous coating of the stomach and bowels. This would lead to friction and irritation of passing hard masses which often set up cancers and tumours. If despite any treatment or avoidance of recognising the issue the cancer had gone too far then Dr J Collis Browne's Chlorodyne was an excellent palliative for both tooth ache and cancer.

Of course the cause of cancer was unknown and Dr Elizabeth Garrett Anderson, in 1897, noted that English and foreign specialists were trying in vain to discover a cure. But there were discussions about the potential causes of cancer. In 1879 a paper by a Dr Budgett on tobacco stated that there was evidence tobacco smoking was a fertile source of disease affecting lips, tongue and respiratory passages and that the cancers were four times more likely in men than women and the findings of the cancer hospital supported this. In 1892 a Dr Parker supported this saying that he hated smoking saying, from end to end it was a nuisance. It ended in cancer, apoplexy, bankruptcy, bad temper and hydrophobia. It was an invention of the devil and it should be noted that no dog smokes nor does any bird. However if you did smoke you could do no better than use Condy's fluid as a mouth wash after using stale tobacco. It would instantly remove all tastes and odours from the mouth and breath and prevent sore lips which often caused cancer. It only took another 150 years to prove their conclusions were correct.

Another particularly unpleasant cancer that was identified was chimney sweeps cancer otherwise known as soot wart which was actually a squamous cell carcinoma of the skin of the scrotum and it was thought it affected 2000 people in the country and was described as a most frightful disorder with cases in boys as young as eight years old. Aside from the risk of the cancer the boys had to have the skin on their knees and elbows hardened by rubbing with strong saline solution in front of a hot fire being 'encouraged' to accept the treatment with a cane or bribery. Despite this they often came back down the chimney with bleeding knees and elbows and soot wart.

In 1896 the golden age of civilisation was wished for. A time when there would be enough for each person and there would be domestic happiness. The three great cancers eating out the vitality of modern life – gambling, intemperance and pauperism – would be eliminated.

If you had cancer and refused treatment or treatment was not working you might wish to live out your time in comfort. In 1898 a home of comfort for patients in the final stages of consumption, cancer etc. could be had in St Andrew's Lane, Portsmouth for 10/- to 30/- a week. Closer to home Mrs Crowie's Home at Jevington in 1886 received patients suffering from complaints other homes had rejected such as surgical cases, paralysis or cancer cases. She charged 10s 6d a week for board and lodging and had accommodation for 20 patients with 145 being admitted over a year.

Consumption

*Consumption, so called because it was seen as a wasting disease and, as such was also called phthisis, is scientifically known as tuberculosis. Tuberculosis (TB) is caused by a bacterium **Mycobacterium tuberculosis** which presents itself with a persistent cough lasting three weeks or more that produces blood stained mucus, night sweats, weight loss, fatigue, swellings in the neck and it particularly affects the lungs.*

In 1866 consumption was considered the most fatal disease in Scotland accounting for 12% of all deaths. However the overall low death rate in Eastbourne was also reflected in the numbers of consumption deaths. In 1878 there were 36 consumptive deaths out of a total of 210 in a neighbouring town but in Eastbourne there were only 32 deaths out of a total of 207. A small difference but one considered worth announcing. In 1886 the cause of consumption was thought to be tubercule which was a low vitality substance that was deposited in the lungs. It quickly degenerated causing the lungs to break down and form cavities in them.

Although in 1898 Eastbourne made no special claim to treat phthisis it was suggested that with the marine climate with winds laden with ozone coming direct from the sea and a very equitable temperature as well as great facilities for open air treatment patients might be expected to do well. In 1899 a consumptive who came to Eastbourne spent most of his time out doors on the golf links and with a new system of care was cured. A doctor suggested a person who was "run down" through over pressure of business might be better served by spending a week in Eastbourne compared with a month in Hastings.

The travel to Eastbourne might be considered to be a risk to those free of the disease. In 1892 a problem was identified where, if there was no spittoon in the railway carriage, a coughing patient requiring to expectorate must spit directly onto the mat. The spittle itself was not considered dangerous until it dried at which point the infection would be found floating in the air. The problem being that cleaning the spittle soaked mats was considered to be dangerous so it was seldom done. However for fellow travellers in 1894 neglecting to breathe through the nostrils was an aggravating cause of the consumption that abounded, according to Rev H C Wilson giving a lecture at the Caldecott Museum, especially in young girls. Even with spittoons, presumably, breathing at all in an enclosed railway carriage would be considered a risk.

If the Eastbourne train was considered a risk then consumptives, who could afford it, would often go abroad for the winter. In 1895 the question was what to do with English consumptives when the days were short and the skies cloudy. One of the popular European resorts was Davos, Switzerland but it was reported in the *Medical Press* that there were just as many bacilli in the patients in Davos as there were in the patients in London. Bu there was also the risk of spreading the disease to the local inhabitants who did the laundry for the visitors. Another popular destination was Madeira. In 1865 20 male patients of respectable appearance were sent from the Brompton Consumptive Hospital to a hospital in Madeira for winter residence at a cost of £400. However in 1879 Eastbourne was noted that because of its exceptionally favoured climate it had been steadily growing in public esteem as a winter residence.

If an exotic holiday abroad was beyond the means then like all diseases at the time prevention was better than cure.

In 1862 there was reason to believe that consumption may be a natural consequence of the surfaces (of the lungs) being imperfectly protected in cold weather so that the blood was driven to the lungs. There were also certain errors of diet by which too little animal food and too little fatty matter had been supplied habitually according to the *Winslow Medical Critic*. Butchers who ate large quantities of animal food were, as a body, generally considered to be free from consumption. On the other hand consumptive people were, as a rule, in the habit of abstaining from fat. The answer was fluid fat in the form of Cod Liver oil which was shown as an effectual remedy in the treatment of consumption.

Cod Liver oil was immediately leapt on as the basis for any treatment. In 1867 Moller's cod liver oil won first prize at the Paris Exhibition and was contracted to the North London Consumption hospital as it was the best and purest oil and was considered invaluable in the treatment of consumption. Available for 2s 3d a bottle from Flint's the chemist in Eastbourne. If pure oil was not effective then in 1869 there was Savory and Moor's Pancreatic Emulsion which was panceatized digestive cod liver oil.

Of course if you did not want oil there was plenty of alternatives. Mr Congreve's book on consumption declared the most successful treatment in the world for consumption. His book which was advertised for forty years was available for a shilling, post free. Royalty apparently patronised Ashton Provost's Camphorine which dealt directly with consumption and was the most extraordinary medicine ever discovered for coughs and consumption. A D Harmer of South Street and

Pevensey Road could not compete with this although they offered Harmer's cough, asthma and consumption pills which would prove invaluable. If you wanted safe treatment then Crosby's Balsamic Cough Elixir not only had success in consumption and night sweats but it was free from opium and squills (digitalis).

In 1864, Keating's cough lozenges which effectively cured incipient consumption and proved prevention was better than cure. As always there was the ever present J Collis Browne's Chlorodyne but also agents in South Street, Seaside Road and Susan's Road offered Alofa's safe herbal remedies whose ointments could treat ringworm or piles, whose tinctures could treat consumption and special feminine disorders and who offered a line of hair restorer.

There were other elements to 'consumption' that were of interest. It was reported that in 1842 the annual consumption of tea was one and a third pounds per head but by 1862 this had increased to two and two third pounds per head due to the taxes being reduced. The Treasury noted that despite the taxes being reduced the overall tax intake had risen due to the increased purchasing of tea. While sipping their tea it was noted that the annual consumption of coal in 1861 was 83 million tons and this was expected to rise to 2,000 million tons by 1961, a hundred years forward and at that rate the British coal reserves would be exhausted by 2000. Climate change activism was not quite so developed at the time. Sir George Strickland announced in 1862 that the increased consumption of tobacco increased the rate of insanity. If you wished to reduce the consumption of gas then dealers E Pierce and son of 28 Pevensey Road could supply the Welsback system of incandescent gas light that trebled the light of ordinary burners and halved the gas consumption. It was superior to electric light and one eighth the cost.

Corpulency

The state of being grossly fat or overweight. Currently a person is considered overweight if they have a Body Mass Index (BMI) of 25 or over. If it is over 30 then the person is considered obese. Alternatively if a man has a waist size of over 94cm or a woman has a waist size of over 80cm they are considered overweight. Being overweight has the potential for the development of type II diabetes, strokes or coronary heart disease.

With low and potentially infrequent wages as well as large families it is perhaps surprising there would be a problem with obesity in the Victorian era but a problem there was.

In 1863 it was considered that a well constituted adult should not have more than about a twentieth of the whole body being fat. Although this might be exceeded to a certain extent without inconvenience it would become a regular disorder when it reached the proportion of a half. The downside being that, in general, obesity was not considered to be accompanied with longevity. Most fat people were considered of plethoric habit with the functions of the vital organs being always, more or less, impeded.

In 1890 the *Family Physician* noted that obesity was not peculiar to any particular period of life although age exercised a considerable influence on the production of fat with children being, relatively, fatter than adults. It also observed that females were more predisposed to obesity than men and women who had never borne children seemed more frequently affected than those who had several pregnancies. Over feeding was seen, in the majority of people, to induce fat as would the habit of taking a great deal of drink though it be only water. The *Source of Health* in 1884 identified that obesity was the result of more consumption of fat, sugar and starch than the system required. Years before fast food was implicated.

The difficulty where women were concerned was highlighted in an article by Publicola in the 1887 *Eastbourne Gazette* although in brackets there was a disclaimer stating that their views were not always endorsed by the editor. The issue was the latest fashion which was to dispense with the corset allowing the figure to assume an unaided outline. The question was asked; can anything be so ugly? Corsets, properly used, had the merit of confining a too redundant supply of adipose tissue. It was suggested that our lady friends with a tendency to obesity would look hideous.

The overall impression was that men did not need to worry about corpulence but if women really wanted to abandon the constraints of a corset how could they get rid of the over-supply of adipose tissue? Of course there was no end of help out there.

As always there were the solutions that could be sent for and paid in stamps. In 1886 a one hundred page book with recipes and notes on how to harmlessly, effectually and rapidly cure obesity without semi-starvation could be bought for 8 stamps. If followed the effects would not merely reduce the amount of fat but by affecting the source of obesity it would induce a radical cure of the disease. Without identifying the source it also medicalised the issue. If you could only afford six stamps you could obtain a valuable treatise showing how fat could be destroyed (not merely lessened). This could be achieved easily, pleasantly without hardship or nauseating drugs with the certainty of cure.

If medication was what was required Dr Cameron's valuable pills were positively the only certain remedy for stoutness and obesity. They were guaranteed harmless although one would wonder why anyone would take anything that was positively harmful. The cure was rapid, permanent with no starvation and a graceful figure could be quickly restored. On application the height and weight should be stated and 2s 6d or 4s 6d included for a wonderful scientific discovery.

Should harmlessness be a priority then in 1891 Dr Densmore contended that the natural food of man was fruit and nuts and he was very successful in curing obesity but there were other ways of losing fat. Taking the waters in Marienbad, a spa town in the Czech Republic with curative carbon dioxide springs, was recommended by a French doctor, M Schindler. If you wanted to stay at home then in 1893 a hospital trained masseuse would visit ladies, gentlemen and children successfully treating paralysis, rheumatism, face ablutions and obesity but if you wanted electricity that would be extra. If you could not afford electricity Miss Thornbjorn of 17 Gildredge Road who was fully qualified in massage and Swedish manual treatments would attend cases of nerve disease, heart disease, general weakness and obesity.

Obesity could also be fun. The question in 1882 was: how can a long word of four syllables be spelled with four letters? Answer: OBCT (Obesity)

Diabetes

Diabetes is a disorder where the body is unable to break down glucose into energy due to the absence, either total or partial, of the hormone insulin which is produced by the pancreas. This results in high levels of blood sugar and numerous physical manifestations such as loss of sight, ulcers and gangrene. There are now two types of diabetes known: Type 1 – where the body's immune system attacks the Islets of Langerhans, the bodies in the pancreas that produce insulin resulting in no insulin being available to the body. Type 2 – the body does produce some insulin but not enough to control the glucose levels with one of the main causes being corpulency. Although diabetes was recognised as a disease it was not until 1889 that Joseph von Mering and Oskar Minkowski found that dogs who had their pancreas removed developed diabetes. It was not until the early 1900s that Jean de Meyer and Sir Albert Sharpey-Schafer identified that the Islet of Langerhan, which had been discovered by Paul Langerhan in 1869, produced insulin. The link between insulin and diabetes was not established until the 1920s.

Medical men in the Victorian era were able to diagnose a disease called diabetes and recognised many of the effects that were displayed by the afflicted but there was no understanding of the cause or, of course, the treatment but there was no shortage of offers.

In 1878 you could avail yourself of the Hall's Medicated Voltaic Electric perforated plasters which were sold as a curative agent unsurpassed by any medical discovery of the century with its benefits being sometimes, (a significant get out clause) almost (another one) miraculous. It could be used for strains and bruises, nervous pain of the bowels, cricks, sharp pains in the breast and diabetes. Despite the claim that a single trial could be convincing the medical commonality between a bruise and diabetes is difficult to understand.

If electric plasters were considered a little extreme then Du Barry's delicious Revalenta Arabica food that renewed blood and treated all kinds of fevers, noises in the head, low spirits, waterbrash (mixing of large amounts of saliva with stomach acids resulting in a bad taste in the mouth and heart burn), sea sickness, epilepsy and diabetes. Again the range of efficacy from sea sickness to diabetes is impressive. But, as with all things medicinal *caveat emptor* – be wary of being cheated with worthless substitutes. Only the genuine article would suffice. An acknowledgement to diabetes though suggested that if the

Revalenta biscuits were required by a diabetic they should mark their order "*without sugar*".

Unsure about treatment? Then consult the *Family Physician* which contained useful information to those who would want to know anything of the two commonest disorders incidental to humanity: Disease of the Ear and Diabetes. Perhaps small pox and diphtheria might have been of more concern to the readers although perhaps ear ache was more common.

If not the *Family Physician* then patients could educate themselves with the *Smith's Domestic Encyclopaedia or Household Guide* for sixpence. As well as how to treat diabetes it would also give helpful advice on the most worrying afflictions like chapped hands, ear ache, bruises, freckles, how to remove hair from the face, how to grow hair on the bald spots and how to make raisin wine. It was full of simple and inexpensive methods of cure.

While reading any of the very helpful guides a diabetic could improve their condition by sipping Bethesda anti diabetic water from Waukesha in the USA. Assuming you had bought the genuine article with the Bethesda label it would treat diabetes, Bright's disease, dyspepsia and all derangements of the liver and kidney. Alternatively *Modern Medicine* could recommend water charged with carbonic gas (soda water) which would lessen the sense of ravenous hunger which should be remembered when dealing with cases of diabetes.

Epilepsy

This is a condition affecting the brain with bursts of electrical activity causing the person to experience seizures which might express themselves as uncontrolled fits, stiffness or collapse. It can start at any age and is lifelong but with proper control those with epilepsy can live a normal life going to school and getting employment.

Epilepsy was certainly considered to be a significant illness but it was aligned towards being a mental condition rather than a physical one. In 1880 the *Family Physician* drew a distinction between a fainting fit which might be brought on by a trivial event like being in a hot room or a long abstinence from food and epilepsy, or *petit mal,* which could come on momentarily and without any exciting cause. Also, in epilepsy the heart was seen to beat faster and the pulse can be felt at the wrist but the patient in a faint would have almost no pulse.

In 1895 epilepsy was described as a most dreadful of all complaints but an advert for a certain cure, without fear of failure, was offered by an anonymous advertiser who offered full instructions for a cure. Dr Richardson suggested in 1886 that perhaps people who discovered they were not geniuses should not be discouraged as he declared genius was a form of epilepsy. On the other hand idiocy was a passport to incarceration in an asylum.

Naturally there was competition to be the cure for epilepsy. In 1863 a Caithness ancient cure was described and this required the sufferer to drink from a cup that was the skull of a suicide victim. Perhaps if that was extreme there was always Dr J Collis Browne's Chlorodyne which would effectively cut short all attacks of epilepsy as well as curing the numerous other maladies it claimed it was capable of. If money was tight or if the sufferer was a little suspicious they could, in 1896, go for H G Root's offer of a bottle of his remedy for nothing, to try before paying any money. Root claimed to have made a life-long study of epilepsy and St Vitus' Dance and when he said he could cure epilepsy he meant he could offer a radical cure and that because others might have failed to cure that was no reason not now receiving a cure. As it was almost certain the remedy would not cure epilepsy one wonders if he actually ever received any payment. Whether Mr Root counted as one of the 'foreign quacks' that Mr Williams of London in 1885 warned people of is unknown but sufferers of fits, epilepsy and falling sickness were warned they should not entertain the idea of consulting with them but to consult with him instead after all he was a specialist with 30 years' experience.

Aside from the selection of treatments epileptics were also offered degrees of accommodation. This might be being cared for at their home despite it, potentially, being difficult. An advertisement in the Eastbourne paper in 1889 wanted an old musical box to amuse an epileptic imbecile boy of 9 years whose only safety was a padded room. He lived in Langney Road and his parents were not concerned about the appearance of the toy only that the cost should be reasonable.

If home was not an option then rooms in Jevington might be required. In 1895 terms for a lady suffering at times with epilepsy were 10s a week although she was able and willing to give service in part payment. In addition she was a good needlewoman. A permanent home was required for a gentleman with epilepsy in 1889 with board and residence for £35 per annum. There was a home in Jevington where in 1886 every effort was made to secure the freedom and comfort of home life to the inmates. Of the 76 patients 12 were epileptics, 2 were mental inmates and 2 deaf and dumb.

There were also homes for epileptics such as the one run by Mrs Emily Crowie in Myrtonville, Polegate in 1888 which was opened in 1887 and had rooms for 20 residents only 5 minutes from the station. Mrs Crowie, a widow and matron also ran the home for epileptics and invalids at Winton House in Pevensey bay.

Hospitalisation was also an alternative and in 1876 the Guardians provided accommodation for epileptics, the aged and infirm at the work house. Provision gradually improved there with the opening of the Epileptic Hospital which was later converted to the children's hospital. The Guardians were also given permission by the Local Government Board to send a girl to the Training College for Epileptic Children at Lingfield, Surrey (1890-1902) which specialised in training and educating epileptic children to try to live a normal life.

In 1873 there was also the National Hospital for the Paralysed and Epileptic which was established in 1859 and had branches around the country. But there was a much darker side to the hospitalisation of epileptics and that centred round the uncertainty of the causes of the disease. In 1896 the Sussex County Lunatic Asylum there were 146 male and 187 female inmates with a few idiot children and of those 94 were epileptic patients who, together with the suicidal patients, were kept under 24 hour supervision. Once the Hellingly Asylum was opened there was also a high number of epileptic patients in their care.

Hay Fever

Hay fever is an allergic reaction to pollen affecting the nose, mouth and throat. There is no cure and no effective way of preventing it but it is, generally, not fatal.

Hay fever was first identified by John Bostock a self-taught medical man from Liverpool who could only find 28 other people who had the same affliction as himself. Although he tried many 'cures' including opium he found greatest relief in residing in a summer house in Ramsgate. Fresh sea air, as was abundant in Eastbourne became a popular remedy for hay fever although it did not stop the *Times* reporting that the Duke of Devonshire had hay fever in 1827.

The fact that Bostock could not find a cure did not stop others claiming they had. If you had hay fever in 1881 then Dunbar's Alkaram was offered as the only cure ever discovered for hay fever. If it was used during the hay season it would ward off all attacks and cure all cases of hay fever in 10 minutes.

Alternatively Glykaline in 1894 rapidly relieved hay fever and was the quickest surest and safest remedy. However the new fashionable anaesthetic – cocaine was considered to be destined to be the most useful drug in the pharmacopeia. Injected into the gums it was claimed to remove sensation as completely as laughing gas. In particular it had been tried with very marked success in the alleviation of the troublesome malady hay fever.

Before embarking on using cocain (*sic*) for hay fever more could be learned about the illness in 1891 by reading *Medical Essay Volume III* which covered: how to judge wholemeal bread, how to keep warm, how to live 100 years, how to become beautiful and attractive as well as everything you needed to know about flatulence and hay fever.

Hysteria

In the Victorian era hysteria was considered very common especially among women. Hysteria was derived for the Greek for the word 'womb' and the disorder was linked to women's reproductive systems. Although women and police constables often carried smelling salts or *sal volatile* made from ammonia to be used for women who 'fainted' or 'swooned' the affliction could be considered so serious that people could be committed to asylums.

The newspapers often reported suicides that were linked to hysterical episodes. One in 1893 was an inquest on a suicide in Avalon House which was variously described as a private lunatic asylum or a medical boarding house. It was suggested that the victim was not hysterical but was quite mad although the line between hysteria and madness was considered not to be very distinct. There was a certain degree of distinction in 1884 when a lodging house tenant in 25 Cavendish Place was reported to have been subject to hysteria brought on by drink. Indeed it was claimed she was never sober a day. When a promised turkey did not arrive on time the land lady who was supposed to have delivered the bird received a black eye from the tenant who was later fined £5 for the assault and £1 1s for the broken furniture. It must be assumed that more than one punch was thrown in the altercation.

If you were unclear about hysteria in 1899 the Viavi lectures at the Eastbourne Town Hall were on "Hysteria and Insomnia as a result of Internal Derangement". The British Viavi Company with an office set up in 49 Terminus Road in 1898 by a Miss O'Dowda held a wide range of drawing room lectures on a wide range of health issues for ladies in Eastbourne and Bexhill. Their subjects were primarily on health and hygiene and as Miss Glassford who presided over all the country's offices noted they always attracted a good audience.

Once the ladies knew exactly what hysteria was they could turn to Du Barry's Revalent Arabica food in 1878 and Dr Collis Browne's Chlorodyne in 1869 because they cured hysteria as well as every other disease known to man or woman.

More specifically in 1874 there was a *Guide to the Cure of Debility* by Dr Henry Smith who gave prescriptions and instructions for the cure of all diseases including noises in the head, indecision (not sure if that was a disease), blushing (not usually a fatal disorder), self- distrust, love of solitude, groundless fears and hysteria all for two penny stamps.

For hands on treatment then you could try Kreutzberg's massage and electrical treatment for rheumatism, gout and hysteria all cured in a short while. An examination was free when they attended Eastbourne every day. Sufferers from hysteria would be prescribed the Weir Mitchell treatment for which there was special accommodation in Heathfield. Weir Mitchell was an American neurologist who pioneered rest cures for hysteria. The patient would be isolated, confined to bed given electrotherapy and massage and put on a full fat diet that might include drinking up to 2 quarts of milk a day.

If any milk was left over they could wash down Dr William's Pink Pills for disorders such as paralysis, impoverishment of the blood, all forms of female weakness and hysteria. They were definitely a tonic and definitely not a purgative just in case you were confused.

Pneumonia

Pneumonia is a lung infection that can be caused by a bacteria, virus or fungi. It inflames the alveoli or air sacs in one or both lungs filling them with pus or phlegm which results in coughing and breathlessness. It was often seen to shorten the period of a primary illness in those patients already considered moribund leading it to be called "the old man's friend".

In 1886 there was a distinction made between bronchitis which was considered nothing more than a bad cough with some fever and a possibility of difficulty in breathing and pneumonia that showed severe fever, more pain and difficulty in breathing and, generally, the expectoration was rather of a red colour. The patient was advised to be put in a warm room. Unusually for the time it was considered that medicine was not of much use. It was actually of not much use in any of the illnesses the Victorians were subjected to but it was unusual for it to be admitted there was little in the way of effective medication. Stimulants were also considered unnecessary but rest, warmth and large quantities of linseed poultices to the chest, nutritious but light food such as milk, soup and bread and milk and, especially for children, an atmosphere of steam was all important. The disease was considered to be serious and it was noted that it could spread through carelessness or neglect.

A serious disease it was and in 1897 of the 521 deaths recorded in Eastbourne 249 were males dying, mainly, of pneumonia, inanition (exhaustion through lack of nourishment) and violence with 272 women dying mainly of influenza, cancer, old age or convulsions. Previously in 1889 an investigation had shown that men over the age of 25 and an intemperate use of alcoholic beverages cut 10 years of their life and greatly increased deaths from pneumonia, pleurisy and epilepsy.

As there was no effective treatment prevention was the order of the day. In *1892 Cassell's Saturday Journal* suggested that as pneumonia was the deadly foe of old age every precaution known to modern medicine should be taken even to stopping in bed until the room was of the proper temperature which did not seem a particularly scientific recommendation. In 1899 it was observed that only 10% of people breathed properly. The proper way to breath was through the nostrils and not the mouth as the nostrils filtered and warmed the air before it reached the lungs and caused pneumonia.

Possibly ignoring the advice that pneumonia could not be treated Scott's emulsion in 1896 was held to be a wonderful cure that fed the blood with essence of nourishment and was effectual in the cure of pneumonia. As with all medicines it was important to ensure the genuine article was used and this was identified by the trademark of a man carrying a fish on his back on the wrapper.

Protection was the key and there were lectures about protecting oneself from pneumonia – tickets from the Medico Electric institute 126 Terminus Road – by the wearing of the Kelley Magnetic nerve invigorator.

Scrofula

Scrofula or cervical tuberculosis lymphadenitis is an infection in the lymph nodes in the neck caused by the bacterium **Mycobacterium tuberculosis** *causing chronic, growing mass in the neck that presents with fever, chill, and weight loss. It was also called the King's Evil because it was thought it could be cured by the touch of royalty.*

In 1885 Dr Fussell the Medical Officer in Eastbourne was busy touting the health giving benefits of the dry and bracing air of Eastbourne and advising invalids in the early stages of scrofula that they could enjoy the benefits of a sojourn in the town. If one of the treatments for scrofula was identified the explanations of the causes were many and various.

In 1896 a generalised cause of what was described as one of the wasting diseases of the scrofulous or consumptive types which were closely related was a germ. In scrofula the germ was in the blood and manifested itself in swellings and open sores while in consumption the germs were seated in the lungs. However, it was thought that both diseases resulted from an impoverishment of the blood and the resulting loss of flesh, weakness and emaciation. This had been the view in 1895 when consumption, St Vitus' dance (rapid, uncontrolled, uncoordinated jerking of the hands, arms and feet), rickets and scrofula were all traced to low vitality caused by poor nourishment. The body was unable to assimilate food and a gradual decline of vital force was inevitable. Nourishment of a more specific sort was identified by Mr William Cobbett and Dr Corrigan in 1863 who claimed the potato, the curse of Ireland and the national food, was the cause of scrofula. They pointed out that the disease did not exist in flesh and fat eating nations. There had been no cases in New Zealand until Captain Cook had substituted the potato for fish and pig flesh in their former foods. However a butcher in Tunstall in 1883 was fined £20 with costs or three months imprisonment for exposing for sale the carcass of a pig which had suffered from scrofula. Whether nutrition played a role of not a more extreme cause was identified by Dr Forbes-Winston in 1884. He claimed that many children contracted scrofula, St Vitus' dance and other diseases through overcrowding in elementary schools a situation which, he thought, was such a cruel system that a worse one could not have been devised.

Of course a popular issue at the time was the case against vaccination for small pox and the anti-vaccination lobby was quick to report that in 1882 *The Glasgow Herald* suggested that 15 diseases including syphilis, small pox and scrofula were disseminated by the practice of vaccination. This was followed up in 1883 by the Anti Vaccination Congress in Paris which showed that not only did vaccination not reduce the death rate and that it afforded no protection against small pox but it did cause a large increase in infant mortality falsely registered as death by scrofula. Indeed it was quite a cause of death in children. In 1878 there were 655 deaths attributed to scrofula in the under one year age group with internal scrofula of tabes accounting for 2270 with 1355 accounted for with syphilis.

However scrofula was caused the pharmaceutical industry was, as always, ready to provide the cure. Just to be on the safe side Swift's Specific treatment of 1887 was an entirely vegetable based preparation containing no mercury, potash, arsenic or other poisonous substances and it had cured hundreds of cases of scrofula. If you were particularly keen to avoid mercury then Bagley's Purifying pills of 1878 were advertised as being one of the best purifying medicines ever brought before the public. It contained the extracts of two of the most powerful stomachic and antibillious herbs known to the botanical world and was ideal for people suffering from boils, worms, scurvy and scrofula. To be more specific then Dr Robert's Pilulae antiscrofulae or alternative pills had been curing scrofula and leprosy for sixty years.

But if you were humble of hearth then you could do no better than use the wonderful Holloway pills of 1876. They worked as well in the humble hearth as they did in houses of comfort and wealth. They were considered the best remedy in the world for female irregularities, tic-douloureux (painful stabbing pains in one side of the head), venereal affections, worms and scrofula. Used in conjunction with Holloway's powerful ointment which had been duly fomented with warm water would quickly remove depraved tumours of the body even scrofulous ulcers and foul sores however old or inveterate.

As always though users were warned to be careful of imitations. In 1878 Pepper's Quinine and Iron tonic could treat scrofula, flatulence and fevers of all kinds but only if the label had J Pepper in red ink. If it did then it could also animate the spirit.

Eastbourne Health – Constipation

The introduction of this book lists a number of very significant health care procedures that were not available to Victorian Eastbourne folk but perhaps never having them and not knowing about them was not really an issue. The fact that the whole population was frequently threatened with potentially fatal diseases like cholera and small pox without any hope of effective treatment might have held the town's attention. It is perhaps interesting that with such dangers abounding that one of the health issues that attracted so much attention, not to mention so many advertisements for 'cures' was the relatively innocuous condition, constipation.

In 1886 it was noted that it was important to distinguish between constipation which was considered to be a relatively unimportant matter treated by various aperients and obstruction which was considered a dangerous state aggravated by the use of aperients. In either case, if there was severe pain, the best first aid while waiting for a medical man was the use of opium used in the same way as if treating peritonitis.

In 1889 the hospital noted that although constipation was one of the minor ills of the town it occupied a prominent place in the population's consciousness. The causes of the disorder ranged from the specific to the very general. In 1865 one of the dangers of constipation were attributed to the ingestion of lead. Painters were accused of eating their dinners with unwashed hands presumably coated in lead containing paint.

The file cutter was observed wetting his fingers and thumb while handling the lead for the dipper. Both brought about a saturnine poisoning which could be fatal. Perhaps more commonly in 1889 constipation, indigestion and dyspepsia was put down to poisoning from partially digested food which entered the circulation with the blood depositing it in joints and muscles eventually also causing rheumatism.

With most of these observations an advertisement for a cure was added. If the blood depositing food around the body was an issue then Siegel's syrup would correct the digestion and break the link between rheumatism and constipation.

Perhaps more commonly constipation was put down to folk having a sedentary life style with a want of exercise, inaction or sluggishness of the liver or an injudicious diet. But the most common cause of constipation was the resistance offered to calls of nature. The putting off until a more convenient 'season' of an absolutely necessary function sowed the seeds of constipation. The use of the word 'season' in 1889 might well explain the problem. If one put off the June call of nature until the autumn or the December call to summer the delay might well explain constipation. Assuming that the delay might not have been so severe then Frazer's Sulphur pills were recommended especially if piles were involved. They were also a good treatment for children as they had a pleasant taste an attractive appearance.

Perhaps Andrew's dandelion, camomile and rhubarb pills for flatulence, indigestion and constipation bought from the chemist in Pevensey Road or Carlisle Road in 1889 would be effective as well as being pleasantly tasty. Carter's pills in 1899 did not claim to be tasty but one a night would absolutely cure sick headache, furred tongues, torpid livers and constipation. They were a small pill at a small price with a small dose.

If you were after effectiveness rather than taste then the 1879 Holloway pills acted as a cleansing agent removing irritant matter from the 'interesting' canal relieving spasms, cramps, painful griping and constipation. Ladies of all ages could turn to Kaye's Worsdell's pills especially if they had constipation and the 1887 Fleming's quinine and camphor pills could be taken by ladies at all times especially if they were irritable, depressed or suffered constipation.

Of course one had to be careful that any medicines taken did not, themselves, cause constipation. Fortunately Bravais' dialysed iron tonic was a pure and simple tonic made from pure iron and oxygen combined without acid. It had all the good effects without producing constipation or turning the teeth black. Quite a bonus.

If any form of medication was to be avoided then massage in 1891 from Brocklesby House in Devonshire Place was offered for paralysis, general debility or constipation. A slightly more exotic treatment was available from 31 Lushington Road. Charles Mackenzie, Practical Acetopath and masseuse offered acetopathy, external application of dilute acetic acid, which could cure asthma, bronchitis, hysteria and constipation.

Diet was noted as being an issue so perhaps the 1881 Maltine, an extract of malted barley, wheat and oats would be the solution. Not only was it important for use in constipation but it also increased weight and flesh in most persons of a thin habit particularly if they were delicate females.

Eastbourne Health - Convalescent and Nursing Homes

With the natural benefits such as the sea, clean pleasant air, invigorating walks along the promenades or the Downs, careful urban design with wide, tree lined street and elegant buildings and, perhaps most importantly a superior drainage and sanitation system with clean water supplies Eastbourne was able to build a first class reputation as a resort that not only attracted holiday visitors but also those recuperating from disease or those wanting to maintain their health. With the arrival of the railway in 1849 there was a ready and wealthy clientele living in the crowded, dirty and frequently disease ridden metropolis of London. Much of the care and convalescence industry in Eastbourne was aimed at that market. As early as 1864 the Eastbourne Convalescent Institution for the benefit of the sick poor of London solicited help from the visitors of Eastbourne, the pleasant watering place, who were enjoying the blessings of the pure bracing air. Besides money they would gratefully accept donations of old linen, clothes and books. As almost an afterthought to the local residents the institute offered to accept cases of accidents in the town providing there was a vacancy. An appeal for contributions in 1893 by the Ladies Samaritan Society of the National Hospital for the Paralysed and Epileptic sought funds for the purpose of sending convalescent patients to the country and seaside. They hoped that those enjoying the health giving breezes of Eastbourne would think of and help the poor sufferers who could not possibly renew their strength in the airless and crowded homes (in London) where they languished. But attracting large numbers of people recovering from disease but potentially still infected was not without risk. In 1871 there was concern that the consistently low death rates in Eastbourne would be adversely affected by numbers of people lodging in Eastbourne to recover from their ailments only to succumb to them thus elevating the overall death rate. It was considered a great success for Eastbourne that there did not seem to be an increase in death rate due to the visitors. However care still had to be taken. In the same year lodging house keepers were reminded to be alive to adopting measures to prevent their houses being made into convalescent hospitals of infectious disease without prior knowledge. It might be considered that those suffering from the many and various infectious diseases did not necessarily know how they were transmitted or when they stopped being infectious. The proprietors were reminded that if they did have an infected person stay they had to disinfect the property and have it certificated before they could reopen.

One of the issues with convalescent homes in the earlier days was that no-one really knew how many there were or what sort of accommodation they offered, what class of clientele they were suitable for or what their costs were. It was proposed there would be a list compiled. This might have been relevant for the more stable establishments but there appeared to be an amount of volatility in the market. Locally there were a number of private homes advertising. In 1872 a private convalescent home in Twyn House Seaford offered families accommodation with or without board and the benefit of sea water in the home. A new convalescent home was opened in Seaford in 1891 and this boasted large, lofty rooms with exceedingly picturesque views. Quite whether the clients appreciated this was not stated as the home specialised in the reception of 8 to 10 children between the ages of 2 and 12 whose "young lives had been chequered with illness and who needed careful nursing and bracing air". In 1887 a furnished home with 2 sitting rooms, 5 or 6 bedrooms and a kitchen was required for 6 weeks somewhere in the Sussex countryside for a few convalescent children from a Cripple's home near London. A garden or orchard was considered essential.

Locally there was a choice of establishments. In 1894 47 Seaside was for letting being described as suitable for a boarding house or convalescent home having tea gardens by the sea and 24 rooms one being 37 feet long for the rental of £100.

In 1887 there was Shaftesbury House in Seaside. In 1898 patients were received by the Misses Holman from any physician or surgeon into a comfortable nursing home in 27 Hyde gardens. Suitable for convalescents, chronic, medical, maternity or surgical cases with home comforts and every attention all for 3 guineas. The Invalids nursing home run by S Meech in 1888 offered massage by a medical rubber (masseur), his wife who was also a lady rubber, offered to attend patients at their residence or at their home originally in 4 Park Terrace, St Leonards Road but after 1889 at Wandsworth House, 93

Tideswell Road. Invalids could find comfortable apartments as long as they were not mental cases at 11 Wilmington Square in 1892. Miss Browne at the Redoubt Nursing home 72 to 74 Royal Parade accepted medical, artificial sunlight, convalescent rest cure and others for moderate fees. In 1892 the Eastbourne Nursing institute for Superior Hospital Trained nurses and home for paying patients was run by Miss Norman, the Lady Superintendent in 24 Hyde Gardens. Alternatively there was the Private Nursing Home in 'Lucerne' De Roos Road run by Miss Silver and Miss Richardson (trained at St Bartholomew's hospital) who would receive medical, surgical, operation and massage cases. There was a comfortable home for children of weak intellect well cared for by a trained nurse experienced in mental cases. £100 a year fee in 1891. Applications to Mrs Webb's Registry office, 68 Seaside Road.

Those convalescence homes that did exist could always be improved. In 1898 it was proposed and agreed that the land on which the old iron hospital at the Sanatorium be prepared and made suitable for the convalescents to play skittles. Dr Browne was authorised to purchase a set of skittles.

No matter how many establishments there were there might be room for more. In 1899 the 2nd Sussex Artillery Volunteers pledged to organise a scheme for establishing a convalescent home somewhere on the Royal Parade for the reception of 10 or more soldiers of sailors returning home from the Transvaal in South Africa. Applications were made to the Government for permission to take on one or more houses on the Royal Parade.

Opposing the application it was suggested that the Military Hospital in Ordinance Yard Seaside could be extended but the hospital, despite being staffed with an army medical officer, two non-commissioned officers and two men of the medical staff corps, was considered to provide inadequate accommodation being in the East End, the unhealthiest part of the town. Despite claims that the sanitary conditions were good and the diets, extras and medical comforts being similar to those of all medical hospitals the proposal was rejected. Instead, it was suggested that the All saint's Convalescent Hospital (ASH) should be used instead of going to the expense of hiring, furnishing and fitting up houses on the Royal Parade. The difficulty was that the home was run on particular religious principles. On a somewhat baser level it was pointed out that there were two public houses close to ASH whereas at a home in Royal Parade the convalescents could be kept from such places.

This could be a shame because in 1894 Marza wine was advertised as absolutely the finest tonic pick up being a most palatable scientific iron and coca wine. It was particularly unsurpassed for convalescents after accouchement (giving birth) so perhaps not appropriate for returning soldiers but it was also suitable for athletes, children and all those unstrung, fagged, weary and below par. If you were none of those then in 1896 Coleman's Wincarnis was the finest tonic in the world. It was a preparation of port wine, Liebig's extract of meat and was considered invaluable to the convalescent.

Of course the two biggest suppliers of convalescent care was the All Saints Convalescent Home in Meads and the Homeopathic Convalescent home in Enys Road.

Illustration 4: Nursing Home advertisement

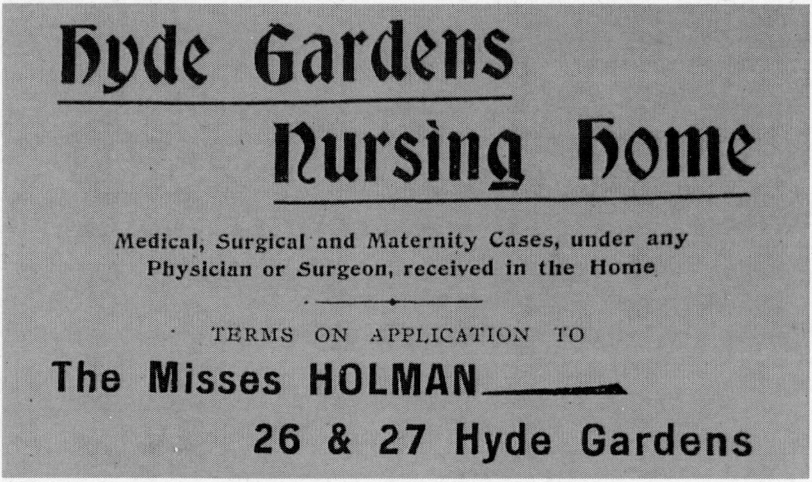

Hyde Gardens Nursing Home

Medical, Surgical and Maternity Cases, under any Physician or Surgeon, received in the Home

TERMS ON APPLICATION TO

The Misses HOLMAN

26 & 27 Hyde Gardens

Eastbourne Homeopathic Convalescent Home

The Eastbourne Homeopathic Convalescent home opened in 66 Enys Road, on the corner of Carew Road opposite the Princess Alice Memorial hospital on August 25th 1888. Doctors Walther and Croucher were involved in the establishment of the home as well as with the homeopathic hospital in Marine Road although the two institutions were separate from each other. The home was founded by Major William Vaughan Morgan with the financial backing of Mrs Clifton Brown and it was closely associated with the London Homeopathic hospital.

It opened with 20 beds, 15 for women and 5 for children. The purpose was to give men, women and children who had recovered from illness the benefit of a temporary Eastbourne home with good food and careful attention from the Matron Miss Lewis and her assistants.

Subscribers could, for one guinea (£1 1s 0d) and donors for 20 guineas have the privilege of recommending for admission one patient yearly for no longer than 3 weeks with proportionate advantages accruing for larger donors or subscribers. At a higher level £1000 or an annual subscription of £50 accorded the donor the endowment of a bed entitling them to having a bed always at their disposal free of any payment. Larger supporters also had a ward named after them.

However before anyone could be admitted they had to be medically certified as not having suffered from any infectious or contagious disease.

The report of 1890 showed that in the half year the home had treated 92 patients compared with 79 in the same half year of the previous year and the cost of each patient was 13s 5d a week. This consisted of 6s 5d on provisions and 7s on general expenses. However it pointed out that subscribers paid one guinea for three weeks stay but as the cost was 13s 5d a week there was a net loss to the home for each patient assuming they stayed the full three weeks (the total cost being £2 10s 3d).

Despite this in 1891 it was proposed that an extension should be built to take men convalescents. By 1894 Enys Road had been renumbered and the home became number 36.

Shortly after the opening though a letter from a local anonymous trader suggested the home was not entirely popular complaining that "hitherto nearly everything has been purchased out of town" and he wanted to know if the managing committee supported local trade. Indeed in the local papers there was little in the way of advertisements for fund raising events certainly compared with the homeopathic hospital so it may be that it was not popular in the town or was more financially self-sufficient.

Although in 1903 by sale of work assistance was invoked towards the Samaritans fund which gave pecuniary aid to poor patients. The sale took place at the home in 36 Enys Road and was conducted by the matron, Miss Waddington, Nurse May and Nurse Edith raising over £22. That Christmas a Pound Day appeal was launched realising, amongst other things 158lbs of tea, coffee, cocoa, sugar, bacon, rice, butter, flour as well as 30 oranges, 12 rabbits and 6 pheasants. To celebrate Christmas Mr Scott (florist of Enys Road) donated a "beautiful" Christmas tree heavily ladened with gifts and ornaments.

In 1901 it was declared that "the benefits to health which patients from the London Hospital must derive from a sojourn in salubrious Eastbourne coupled with the great care and ungrudging attention which they receive at the hands of experienced matron Miss Waddington (Sister Dora) and her able assistant Nurse Amy were inestimable". But in 1935 L J Knowles, Secretary, wrote that "in its modest seclusion at 36 Enys Road the convalescent home has not attracted the attention and support it deserves in spite of the fact it has existed in Eastbourne for 47 years". He went on to say that the admission of patients was not restricted to those who have been treated in hospital (possibly meaning the London hospital to which it was affiliated). Some 25% came from other sources and a few were admitted from Eastbourne itself. Possibly the home was not popular in Eastbourne because it served mainly patients transported down to salubrious Eastbourne from London and not the residents of the town itself. Continuing, he appealed for the gift of a wireless "which would be a boon to patients taking enforced periods of rest".

In 1942 Mr Geoffrey Bowers bought the London Homeopathic Convalescent home, which had been closed for some time, for £4,565 and it became night nurse accommodation for the Princess Alice Memorial hospital.

Illustration 5: Homeopathic convalescence home. Enys Road

All Saints Convalescence Home (ASCH)

A 30 bed convalescence hospital had existed in a handsome building on the Grand Parade for three years prior to 1867 but in that year the Lady Fanny Howard, sister to His Grace the Duke of Devonshire, laid the foundation for the new convalescence hospital situated at the southern end of Meads and close to Holywell sheltered beneath the downs. It was said that a better site for convalescents or invalids of any kind could not be conceived. The aim of the hospital was to provide care for those who had been "cured" of their ills at the large hospitals (there were none in Eastbourne so the hospital was, primarily, catering for people treated in London) but who required gentle nursing care and support for the weeks and months that followed after leaving any charitable institution that had cared for their acute illness. This highlighted the state of post-operative care or treatment for more complex medical cases. An advert in 1866 declared that All Saint's was an institution for the benefit of the sick and poor of London and the country. As with all the charitable enterprises in Eastbourne, of which there were many, perhaps this and the Homeopathic Convalescent home in Enys Road were less popular with the town folk because they catered almost exclusively for Londoners. In 1873 it was suggested that the hospital was not as well-known as it should be as it struggled for funds. There had been 1430 patients in the previous year which was 500 up on the previous and there had still been 100 waiting for admission. Because of this it was being considered either to limit the number of admissions or reduce the amount of food they were receiving due to the increasing cost of gas, water and local rates and the ever increasing cost of coal. It was pointed out that the medical staff never received any remuneration.

The home was to cost £30,000 to build and the full amount was pledged by Mrs Brownlow Byron but only half was accepted with the rest to be raised by other means. Although the existing home at Compton Lodge, listed as being at Hartington Place, had treated 800 convalescents with 30 in attendance at any one time over its short, three year history (1864-1867).

The new hospital was designed to accommodate 100 patients, convalescents and incurables with space for the sisters, their superior and necessary servants and attendants. The building itself was to be built of red brick with Bath stone dressing to the doors and windows. The front section would have two main entrances with two others for accident cases. There was to be a central pavilion divided into two sections with a stair case for men on one side and one for women and children on the other. The design throughout sought to keep men and women separate. From the centre there would be a wing to the south for the sisters and children, ones to the south and north catering for the women and men respectively with offices and the segregated dining halls to the north and the chapel for the inmates to the east. Wards for the men and women would be separate with several day rooms for different stages of convalescence.

By 1869 the building cost had risen to £36,000 but there was now room for 200 patients and 30 incurables and a gate lodge was being added. The establishment was to be run by a Lady Superior and a staff of sisters of mercy belonging to what was denominated as the High Church party. The sisters were said to tend the wounded with oil, wine and cheerful comfort.

It was stated that bringing sufferers from some close court or crowded street where they breathed stagnant air which was perilous to the strong and fatal to the weak to a place where, for a short time, they might enjoy the blessings of pure, invigorating air, good food and careful nursing was a good and charitable act. The fact that it was a charity was a problem in that it required a constant inflow of donations to keep running. It was undoubtedly successful as in 1883 Eastbourne was said to be in full season and the All Saints Convalescent Home was world famous. World famous or not in 1879 it was told to drain its main sewers. But in 1882 all the doctors agreed that during the winter months the iodine and ozone of the sea and the bracing Eastbourne air possessed more invigorating qualities than Devon or the Riviera.

Despite the funding challenge and the numerous fund raising activities the hospital continued to expand. In 1874 the refectories and dining halls were extended and completed, an extra 25 beds were made available because the chapel had been completed and the wards that were being used as a chapel could be reinstated. The chapel itself, called the gem of

Sussex, was 111 feet long, 31 feet 6 inches wide and 58 feet six inches high with room for 300 inmates and it is still in place.

In 1881 a new wing was added with a bright and cheerful sitting room and dormitories for the nursing staff with cloak rooms and toilets. The hospital now claimed to be the foremost institution of its kind in England.

Foremost it might have been but it did not stop the Mother Superior, Miss Caroline Grace Millicent Short asking the Council in 1889 for the "stopping up" of a public short cut across the grounds between South Cliff and Darley Road.

It was also not without its detractors. In 1891 the male patients held a meeting in the library to denounce and refute the false and unpleasant rumours that had been spread by a small number of inmates who despite complaining had wanted to remain in the hospital for their allocated stay. The meeting stated that they had been perfectly satisfied with what they obtained in the hospital; good food and every kindness and attention from all in authority. It was seen as being a home of comfort from the top brick to the bottom; it was beautifully clean and there was all that was to be desired for recovery and health. A glowing testimonial. The home was closed in 2004 and turned into luxury flats. The exterior remains intact as does the chapel.

Illustration 6: All Saints convalescence home.

Eastbourne Health – Cures and Quackery

Without a recognised pharmaceutical industry or even an understanding of disease and treatment let alone a functioning medicines regulatory agency there was ample room for anyone to manufacture and market any type of medicine without any proof of efficacy or even safety. The 'patient', probably self-diagnosing in the absence of affordable medical advice was bombarded with advertisements for revolutionary and miraculous cures for everything from toothache to cancer, from small pox to bunions. Everything was a true remedy, a miracle cure and an invaluable treatment for huge ranges of completely unrelated medical conditions that were eminently affordable. The following is a snap shot of the advertisements for medicines in just one newspaper on just one day in 1881 and is by no means an exhaustive list of 'medicines' available to a trusting and gullible audience:

Goodall's Household Speciality

Quinine wine – best remedy for indigestion, loss of appetite, general debility. Restores delicate individuals to health. Just to prove the medicine manufacturers versatility they also offered Ginger Beer powder, egg powder, Brunswick Black for painting stoves, grates and iron available at all chemists and medicine dealers.

Kaderny's Lumbago and liver pills.

Best pills in the world for ladies' use. Invaluable, best medicine ever offered to the public is a certain and effectual cure for lumbago and liver. Efficacious but does not disorder the stomach or bowels nor unfits anyone from exercise of travelling.

Bethesda Anti Diabetic water

For diabetes, Bright's disease, dyspepsia and all derangements of the liver and kidneys.

Lowe's Pills

A Comfy remedy for indigestion and rheumatism.

Hayman's Balsam of Horsehound

Old and true remedy is the most successful ever offered (which probably is not saying much). Invaluable in the nursery for the relief of coughs in ten minutes.

Himrod's

Cure for asthma, catarrh and colds.

Towle's Chlorodyne

One dose speedily relieves coughs, asthma, bronchitis, consumption, spasms. Invaluable in damp or foggy weather.

Harmer's Seven Cures

There included: Corn and wart solvent, spasmodic and wind drops for chest pain and morning sickness, oceanic saline for face ache and tooth ache, toilet fluid guaranteed not to contain any poisons or injurious drugs for the removal of sunburn or freckles.

Higgin's Anti-Neuralgic powders

All perfectly harmless and never failing for face ache, teeth ache, brow ague, nerve pains.

Dr. Rooke's medicine

Oriental pills, solar elixir for indigestion, asthma, consumption, scrofula and gout.

Crosby's Cough elixir

Free from opium

Pepper's Quinine

Iron tonic strengthens the nervous and muscular system. Animates the spirits

Taraxacun ad Podophyllis

Liver medicine for dyspepsia and biliousness

Dellar's essence for deafness and noises in the ear

Persons for years deaf have heard sounds after a fair trial of Dellar's essence.

Dr. King's Dandelion and Quinine liver pills

Do not contain a trace of mercury. For biliousness, constipation, flatulence, shoulder pain and disinclination for food.

Of course if you did not want to enrich the medicine makers there was always self-help:

Invalid's guide to Positive Eclectic Remedies for Self-Treatment.

Remedies for the cure of all diseases. Every household, man and woman should have a copy. Amongst the guides available were those concerning Worry, Intemperance, Late hours (if that is a disease), Diseases peculiar to women, old age or decay of nature, pimples, impure blood.

Even in minor, real or perceived illnesses or maladies if the patient might be concerned there was always a cure available.

Lockyer's Sulphur Hair restorer

Darkens grey hair, destroys scurf and encourages the growth of hair.

Sulpholine

Cures skin disease like pimples, scurf and roughness as if by magic

Many of the adverts were very insistent that the concoctions were often of purely vegetable matter and contained no poisonous material, no opiates and no mercury, which was a relief, but there must have been plenty of highly noxious substances available to the general public. So many in fact that warnings and treatments for accidental poisoning were printed such as those in 1899.

It stated that everyone knew that bottles containing poisons ought not to be left if the children's way but if they were:

1) If corrosive poisons such as carbolic acid were swallowed the person should be given large doses of oil (not lamp oil) but if no oil was present then any kind of grease or melted butter. (A slight concern because one of the recommended treatments for toothache was the administration of carbolic acid to the tooth).

2) If an irritant or narcotic poison was swallowed emetics of a dessert spoonful of mustard and a pint of water or a handful of salt to a pint of water should be given.

3) For opium poisoning (laudanum) strong coffee or other stimulants as well as an emetic should be given.

4) If phosphorus is injected from sucking matches then barley water mixed with carbonate of magnesia after a good emetic. A doctor might use a stomach pump.

The advice then moved attention to slightly less serious complaints:

5) Irritable chilblains: boil some potatoes with the peel on and use the water as hot as possible dipping the part affected into it for 20 minutes.

6) Relaxed throat: A pennyworth of Stockholm tar (a preparation that was used as a bactericidal especially on horse's hooves) in a jug and pour over one quart of

boiling water. Stir and stand overnight. Bottle and cork it tightly. Use as a gargle night and day swallowing a small quantity if possible.

7) Sick headache: Teaspoon of lemon juice and a pinch or carbonate of soda a quarter of an hour before each meal. Two tea spoonful's of powdered charcoal in half a tumbler full of water for instant relief.

8) Lotion for rheumatism: One gill of best vinegar, half an ounce of cayenne paper, 2 tea spoonful's of table salt. Mix and rub affected parts until a good glow is produced.

The eclectic article also gave advice on how to keep tortoises and how to arrange a child's bed.

Quackery

Every newspaper carried advertisements for a huge selection of miracle cures that, in the main, had no beneficial or curative effects whatsoever. They were mainly based on vegetable matter although as some were quick to point out that they contained no mercury, poisons or noxious materials one might assume that others did contain such matter. At best the 'medicines' had no benefit and at worst they could actually cause harm so it was therefore interesting to note that there was a considerable emphasis on the notion that many medicines were 'quack' medicines. There was obviously considered to be a difference between medicines that had no benefit but were sold with the best of intentions and medicines that also had no benefit but were sold to fleece a trusting and unsuspecting population. There was also a distinction made between those persons who claimed to be medical men, the term medical man often being preferred to the term 'doctor' which implied some degree of medical training or expertise and an actual doctor who had, at least attended medical school. Presumably a 'medical man' was convinced of the efficacy of the medicine he was marketing giving it some credibility despite having no evidence but a quack knew perfectly well that the medicine he was marketing was completely useless and would only benefit his bank balance. The field was, therefore, open to quacks impersonating doctors and quack medicines impersonating although not totally dissimilar to genuine 'medicines' that could be marketed by anyone with a medical qualification or not.

Of course there were those who tried to warn against the use of quack medicines not least those that made medicines and cautioned purchasers against buying imitations that might not have the recognised seal of authenticity the real medicines had. Cooden's pills marketed in 1880 stated that they should not be looked on as quack medicines. They contained un-oxidised phosphorus combined with quinine and other useful but unspecified medicines and were the result of careful scientific investigation by medical men who had made treatment with phosphorus a speciality. If they were for you they were available from Provosts chemist the local agent in Eastbourne

In 1880 the Reverend Barnes Lawrence asked if the numbers of quack nostrums (medicines prepared by an unqualified person and, crucially, are not effective) advertised in the daily papers fairly strike the readers with astonishment? He asked who took all these medicines claiming that it was reckoned that as many pills were swallowed in the country as would fill all the ships in her Majesty's navy and, at the time of Victorian sea power this must have been a considerable number. He commented that it was no wonder the undertakers were thriving. In 1898 people were warned about being led by advertising quacks and fellows who pretended to be able to cure all the ills of the flesh with their pills which, for the most part, contained soap and aloes. But quackery was not to be deterred. In 1865 two quack doctors who became local celebrities after the fashion of Robin Hood were fined 1000 francs in Lille for the illegal practice of medicine. They claimed to be able to cure all sorts of disease *gratis* with the rich paying for them.

It was, perhaps, no surprise that many of the cures were only available through mail order with the purveyors keeping a safe distance from their duped victims. In 1889 a free medical work was available to those suffering from nervous debility. A cure that was free from the aid of quacks from the Institute of Anatomy in Birmingham. In 1875 an altruist who had suffered from nervous and physical debility had cured himself and now, prompted by a feeling of humanity, offered a cure that was not influenced by the quackery of mineral poisons and coloured water. It was a novel and highly successful mode of treatment with a patient test cohort of one. Just send a stamped addressed envelope and you will be sent the details. It may be unkind to describe such offers as scams but the methods seem quite familiar.

If you had tried electricity, ordinary medical men and quackery and none of it had worked for the price of two penny stamps the *Medical Journal* could send you a book that could cure everything from depression, dimness of sight, indigestion, premature decline, consumption and any loss of nerve power which, any of which, if not arrested would end in early death or chronic disease.

The issue for the invalid was to disentangle the hyperbole of the adverts and choose between the medicine that was 'genuine' and did not work and the 'quack' medicine that also did not work.

Eastbourne Health – Deafness

Deafness being a diminution or loss of a sensory faculty was probably not of as much concern to the population of Eastbourne as the scourge of the infectious and often fatal diseases that swept across the country and frequently skirted around the town but it was of some concern to those who lost the facility as much as it was an opportunity for those to assist.

As well as being an impediment deafness could also be used to advantage. In 1882 the directors of the Brighton Railway turned a deaf ear to the many tempting offers of heavy train loads of thirsty and noisy 'Arries and 'Arriets who would find Eastbourne a quiet and sweet place. A definite benefit to those in Eastbourne who disliked the influx of visitors. Councillors at council and board meetings as well as members of the numerous committees that governed Eastbourne were also, frequently, accused of turning a deaf ear to the appeals of the citizens.

There was not a lot of advice about the prevention of deafness but in 1881 it was suggested that to prevent deafness from swimming when particles of water could enter and remain in the ears swimmers should use oiled sheep's wool as ear plugs to keep out the water.

But if despite the oily sheep wool one did go deaf there were plenty of treatments and support to choose from. In 1876 and for many years Deller's Essence was advertised for deafness and noises in the ears. It had, apparently, proved an extraordinary remedy and was strongly recommended by the thousands who had derived great benefit. In addition it was declared to be quite harmless which must have been comforting. Fortunately Orchard's cure for deafness was also described as being perfectly safe containing nothing that could possibly injure the ear. It could be sourced from B K Earnshaw, chemist, who was the Eastbourne agent for $13\frac{1}{2}$ d a bottle. In 1895 the seemingly innocuous Olive Herbal Cure for deafness and earache was available from Olive House in 57 Latimer Road.

But if you did not want to treat your deafness but only wanted to compensate for it there were options. In 1866 the SOUND MAGNIFIER also known as the ORGANIC VIBRATOR was available. It was described as an invisible voice conductor which fitted into the ear and removed the sensation of singing noises in the head. It could afford immediate relief to deaf persons and would enable them to hear distinctly at church and public assemblies. Alternatively Nicholson's Patented Artificial Ear Drums were sold in all civilised countries of the world in 1889. They could cure deafness and noises in the head and were described in detail in a 132 page illustrated booklet.

Those afflicted by deafness, particularly children, could be cared for in the rather intimidatingly named Brighton Institution (others were called Asylums) for the Deaf and Dumb which in 1848 was located in Eastern Road in Brighton and took in deaf children between the ages of 7 and 12 providing they were free from infectious complaints and had either had small pox or had been vaccinated against it. In 1891 they had 50 boys and 39 girls in their care which was 13 more than the previous year. Dr G H Jones a surgeon dentist advertising in Eastbourne announced he was the Honorary Dental Surgeon to the Asylum for Deaf and Dumb females.

In 1892 Dr Barnardo the founder and director of the Homes for Waif, Orphan and Destitute children held a meeting at the Town Hall in Eastbourne. He announced that over the 26 years of its existence it had 20,000 children pass through and they took in blind, hopelessly crippled, dumb and deaf children without hesitation if they were really destitute.

Deafness was not seen as a particular handicap though. In 1887 a rather strange advertisement read that deaf mutes or anyone interested in them were wanted by a Miss D or Avenue Villa, Grand Parade. There were no details as to why they might be wanted. In 1887 an advert asked if anyone could recommend an honest, sober woman (deaf not objected to) to work as a plain cook in a family in Brighton. In 1883 a woman advertised for a situation in Crowborough. She described herself as an elderly person who was a little deaf but this was of no hindrance to her work as a plain, good cook.

When not cooking in 1882 there was an Athletic Sports day held at Devonshire Park by the Deaf and Dumb Teetotal society. It seems a niche society but, nevertheless, there was a band on hand to entertain at least the teetotal section. The courts were also entertained in 1881 when a man who was described as an old reprobate was before the Eastbourne Bench accused of begging, making a loud noise and pretending to be deaf. At the hearing he indulged in a fierce tirade against the Magistrate and police and, for his troubles, he was sentenced, probably verbally rather than in writing, to three months hard labour.

Eastbourne Health - Dentists

Victorian dentistry, as with Victorian medical services was not free at the point of delivery, they were supplied at a cost. Perhaps the cost and the process of dentistry might have been the reason for Mr Shipley Slipper, a London dentist who in 1889 used 10,000 artificial teeth in six months, mainly to his customers from the legal profession had his view of the general public. He claimed that an Englishman never went to a dentist unless he was in pain and after nearly all his teeth were gone. An Englishman wouldn't have a tooth left in his head. Just to offer a modicum of advice he advocated the use of precipitate, although this was not defined, to clean the teeth and not camphorated chalk which made the teeth go yellow.

If the Eastbourne residents were inclined to look after their teeth and spare a visit to the dentist they, perhaps, could use Braggs Charcoal toothpaste which in 1878 whitened teeth and preserved them from decay rendering the gums firm, red and healthy with the bonus of imparting a delightful sensation of freshness unobtainable by any other preparation. But by using the deliciously aromatic DENTIFRICE in Cracrofts Areca toothpaste in 1880 the enamel of the teeth became white, sound and polished like ivory. It, too, was exceedingly fragrant and especially useful for removing incrustations of tartar on neglected teeth. If you preferred the greatest toilet discovery of the age you could do no better than use FLORILINE. In 1889 a few drops on a wet tooth brush produced a pleasant lather which thoroughly cleaned the teeth from all parasites or impurities. There were no details of the parasites that might be lurking between the teeth but Floriline would certainly get rid of them at only 2/6d a tube. If cleaning did not work and you still did not wish to visit a dentist you could, in 1874, employ Bunter's Nervice as an instant cure of toothache giving instant relief and effecting a permanent cure forming a stopping (filling) and healing the tooth. Users were assured it did not injure and was used by dentists and recommended by medical men. If, in 1892, imperfect mastication caused you to suffer from indigestion Mr Shipley Slipper Surgeon Dentist to Caterham College could send you a pamphlet on the painless treatment of the complaint free from observation, gratis and post free on application.

In 1879 in extolling the benefits of the Beckett's Eastbourne Directory it announced that it showed 120 normal streets, roads or places in Eastbourne with 650 named houses and amongst others 9 teachers of music, 16 beer houses, 21 bakers and 2 resident dentists. The emphasis being on resident because, initially, dentists appeared to work as a peripatetic service attending the folk of Eastbourne on occasions. In 1862 Mr Andrew Clark, Surgeon Dentist attended Mr Clayton's Pharmaceutical Chemist in Cornfield Road every Friday from 1 to 4. In 1869 Mr J T Whatford, Mechanical and Surgeon dentist attended for free consultations 51 Terminus Road every Saturday between 11 and 2. As his unique selling point he stated he had been the 1844 pupil of Edwin Saunders who was the Queen's dentist. In 1862 Mr Archibald Sinclair, Surgeon Dentist, attended 5 Cornfield Road on the first and third

Wednesday of each month between 3 and 5 but he boasted his system embraced all the latest improvements and discoveries in dental science although he omitted to say what they were. If you needed dental services you certainly needed a calendar as Mr George Davey, Surgeon Dentist to Lewes Dispensary held consultations at Mr Hall's chemist in Seaside on the first and third Wednesday of each month and he offered several years' experience in the profession and he had a certificate from Guy's Hospital. Mr Dutton's chemist accommodated Mr Richard Slater on the first Thursday in every month between 10 and 4. Although many dentists associated themselves with chemists in 1864 Messers Read could be consulted every Tuesday morning from 9:30 at Mr Butcher's confectioner in Howard house, Pevensey Road. But by 1899 Frederick Wells RDS was a 10 year residential surgeon at 50 Grove road offering his services between 11 and 7 daily. Mr Wells proudly announced he had English, American and Egyptian testimonials and one from His Royal highness the Prince of Wales of equine dentistry. As the premises were so rarely used it is assumed the level of equipment was low and the services of Anthony Harmer of Shaftesbury house in South Road could be accessed at one's own home. Just to hedge his bets he also offered Harmer's toothache essences which gave immediate relief and prevented decay.

But if the tooth paste and the pain relief did not work the visit to the dentist was required. Much of the advertising was centred on extraction of teeth and their replacement with artificial teeth. Little in the way of repair of teeth was seemingly offered although Anthony Harmer offered to stop teeth with gold and silver fitted with care and skill. In 1865 Mr Sinclair offered artificial teeth which were natural in appearance and durable, comfortable and economic and entirely superseded those constructed upon ordinary principles. In 1887 Mr Shipley Slipper was able to fit artificial teeth painlessly without extracting loose teeth or stumps and that the teeth fitted were life like in appearance and could be adjusted without any injurious wires all for 3/6d a tooth or 20s for a complete set. Just in case, he could effect repairs while the patient waited for a trifling cost. There was obviously some price wars as in 1878 Messers Bennett, dentists of 13 Terminus Road offered single artificial teeth for 5 shillings. Acknowledging this Mr Wells did not profess to be the cheapest dentist but he did guarantee his work for five years and he continued his system of supply of artificial teeth upon moderate terms. He would also repair while you waited and, now, he offered painless extractions under nitrous oxide gas for only 5 shillings including the doctor's fees. On the other hand Mr Wells offered ten years guarantee at half the usual charges at the Working Dentist, the Cottage, Grove Road. Just in case the work was not quite so effective Mr Richard Slater in 1862 begged to call the attention of the Nobility, Gentry, Clergy, Visitors and the inhabitants of Eastbourne to CORALINE VULCANITE as a base for artificial teeth which, for accuracy of fit was far superior to the old method of fixing.

A likely disincentive to visit the dentist was that it was not necessarily a painless event so the advent of anaesthesia was seen as a great benefit. In 1884 Mr B L Moseley the Dentists in Regent Street claimed to have used nitrous oxide gas in 45,000 cases and claimed to be the original introducer of the nitrous oxide gas claiming it to be innocuous and even pleasant. Slightly more concerning Mr Moseley now of 27 Terminus Road offered all operations would be perfectly painless using nitrous oxide gas which was the anaesthetic most free from any danger with only one case in a million being fatal. As he also offered ether and cocaine so perhaps a visit to his surgery could be quite an experience.

Hygiene and personal protective equipment appeared to be a second though as in 1895, in Eastbourne, frock coats were worn on weekdays by doctors and dentists to who brown may be a pleasant change after the wearisome black. Female dentists were also a second thought. In 1890 it was announced that London could boast on lady stock broker, 1 lady land scape gardener and 1 lady dentist. None were reported in Eastbourne.

An example of the dentist's sense of humour was an epitaph over the grave of a deceased dentist which read "View this grave stone with all gravity. J_____ is filling his last cavity".

Illustration 7: Dentists advertisement

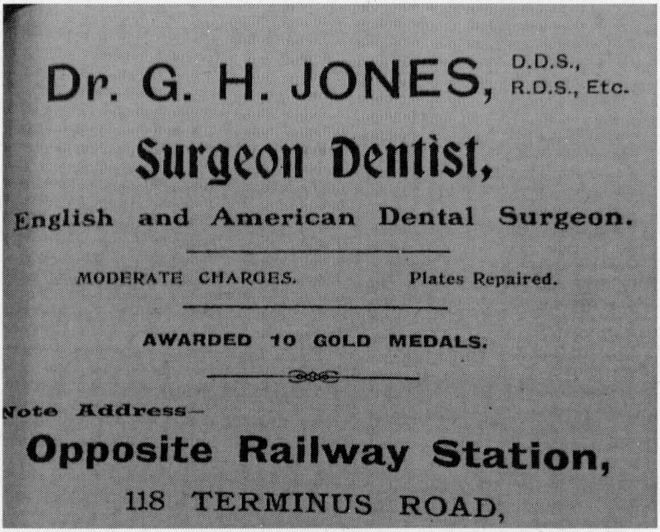

Eastbourne Health – Doctors

In a letter to the *Eastbourne Gazette* in 1878 a writer compared the training required to become a doctor with the training to become a lawyer. In doing so they explained the route to qualification for a doctor. Observing that the time honoured custom of a trainee doctor being apprenticed to a medical practitioner had been in decline for twenty years he explained that the apprentice would previously have paid £200 to £300 to an established doctor for the privilege of being trained but that fee would include his board and lodging. After the expiration of the apprenticeship the student would take a matriculation examination and if successful they would move on to a medical school eventually passing out as a Member of the Royal College of Surgeons with all the medical knowledge he required. This was with the exception of dispensing which was being transferred to chemists with the doctors only prescribing medicines. The new regime would mean that the student would avoid the apprenticeship and go straight to medical school where the fees at the better schools such as Bart's or Guys were 100 guineas a year. During this time the student, as well as studying, would be able to get a staff appointment as a house surgeon, clinical dresser or dispenser at the hospital to help with the fees. They could also attend accouchements.

Once qualified it was observed that the young doctor could easily start up a practice on his own or buy into an established practice as a partner only requiring a little capital to provide subsistence for a time, a few drugs and the wages of an errand boy. This was seen to be a much easier and cheaper progression than the training and subsequent setting up for a qualified lawyer. In addition, once set up, presumably in an area such as Eastbourne, the outdoor life of a doctor was seen to be a much healthier one than being bound to a desk as a lawyer.

In 1862 the life of the hundreds of men who were country doctors was described as being a life spent in unostentatious goodness. They scarcely knew what a good night sleep was and they passed their time in houses of the poor, the abodes of wretchedness and suffering and the haunts of fever and of death. They were men who gave their time and lives for their fellow creatures. Perhaps safety from infectious disease and less than salubrious living conditions working behind a desk with the advantage of a good night's sleep was preferable to some.

The life of a country doctor at least may not have been a very attractive job description but if a female still wanted to become a doctor the concept as well as the passage was not quite as simple as for her male colleague. In 1864 it was pointed out that even after training and qualification if a lady doctor could marry with satisfaction and they could afford it they would. In perhaps a sweeping generalisation it was concluded that they would then leave off doctoring and stick to ordering dinners and watching babies. The object of a lady doctor would be to leave her profession at the earliest possible stage. If she did not marry though she would indisputably gain by being a doctor for she would have the means of earning a livelihood and she would have a perpetual source of interest and occupation.

The gains may be set against the views of the London *Lancet* in 1871 which suggested that female physicians could never be successful at the bedside of patients of their own sex because "women hate one another often at first sight with a rancour of which men can form only a faint conception".

By 1884 things had improved as a letter suggested that there must be delicate cases where refined, modest and sensitive women could have the benefit of doctors of their own sex to whom they could unreservedly explain their complaints and needs.

Whoever trained as a doctor there was no room for complacency as in the summer of 1861 London doctors were complaining about the healthiness of the season. The previous, glorious winter had been the busiest they had known but it had been succeeded by a summer of discontent – and wellness.

Whatever the weather doctors were very often reported as being called out to cases so they must have been doing some good for their patients despite. In 1883 it was being suggested that patients did more for doctors than doctors did for the patients. Calling the doctor was not always the first response to a medical incident though, possibly due to costs that would be incurred. In 1865 a boy was kicked in the shin by a cow and the boy's mother would not call the doctor until she had tried all her own remedies. Eventually the doctor was called and he rubbed embrocation on the leg and bandaged it. On a further visit he found the mother was rubbing the embrocation on the wrong leg. Although this was less than effective the boy was happy about this because rubbing it on the correct leg was painful. Eventually a bone setter was called and they set the bones in the shin right for a fee of ten shillings which was less than the fee a doctor might charge. Eventually bone setters were able to train as surgeons raising their profile to that of the more exalted physician. Another section of the quasi-medical profession that did not progress were the barber surgeons who as well as cutting hair also provide blood-letting services to cure and prevent all sorts of illnesses. They provided a pole for their clients to grip, presumably not when having their hair cut, and this was displayed outside their establishments complete with bandages and collecting bowl as the red and white striped pole recognised today.

A more extraordinary call out was in 1862 when a doctor was called to the Brighton Aquarium where a porpoise had been found to be ill. The doctor prescribed ammonia as a stimulant and, after holding the porpoise in shallow water, the doctor poured *sal volatile* down its throat. Two hours later it was given a dose of brandy and water and put into a small pool where it was observed to be repeatedly banging into the walls. It was diagnosed as being blind and stupid and possibly a bit drunk after the brandy. Needless to say despite the stimulants the creature died.

A doctor's duties were not always so unusual but they could be entertaining. In 1876 a Doctor Lynn was to be found performing sleight of hands at the Devonshire Park Theatre. He performed Palingenesia (the concept of rebirth and regeneration) which was where he appeared to take apart a living man and restore him in instalments. Possibly a version of sawing the lady in half. After the performance he was supposed to be sailing off to India for twelve months. It was not stated whether this was because the trick might not work. Doctors, generally, did not advertise their services but a little publicity would help. Perhaps in place of the travelling Doctor Lynn an Indian Eye Doctor, Dr Carloo was listed as being able to treat a woman in 35 Cavendish Place with a single treatment.

Of course not all of the doctor's activities were quite so acceptable. Over the period there were on going arguments about the benefits of vaccination especially vaccination against small pox. There were vehement arguments against the vaccinations suggesting that far from protecting or curing people of small pox the vaccinations did no good and only infected people with other diseases like syphilis and scrofula. The order of the government to compulsorily vaccinate children exacerbated the matter and doctors did not help. In 1879 doctor J J Gareth Wilkinson was due to speak in Eastbourne although no venue or date or time was published. The title of the talk was to be "Vaccination is the dirtiest villainy practiced on little children". In 1879 the question was why doctors should be allowed to implant dreadful diseases by vaccination? On a slightly more financial slant it was also asked why doctors whose business was to heal the sick would want to prevent ailments? In other words they were doing themselves out of business by vaccinating people and preventing them to succumbing to illness which seemed at odds to the accusation of giving those vaccinated against small pox any number of other serious diseases.

The services of a doctor did not come without cost and payment was not always forthcoming. In 1886 a doctor had to sue an Eastbourne costermonger for 20 unpaid visits at two shillings a visit and for the medicines provided. The patient who tried to defend himself in court was accused of telling woeful untruths and of being deluded. He was ordered to pay four shillings a month to clear the debt.

If you could not afford a doctor then perhaps you could put an advertisement in the paper such as the one that appeared in 1892. It asked if any Eastbourne doctor could receive into his house a lady who, owing to a mental twist, required medical supervision. A reply stating terms would be accepted at the Willard's in Old Town.

There were steps that could be taken to prevent the need for a doctor's visit. In 1877 Epp's cocoa, a delicately flavoured beverage advertised in the *Civil Service Gazette* made simply with boiling water or milk may have saved the doctor's bills and it would help the drinker escape many a fatal shaft by keeping themselves well-fortified with pure blood and a properly nourished frame. With a properly nourished frame you would be able to take the doctor's advice and ensure that your house was free from the germs of disease that doctors agreed were conveyed in the dust found about the home. Beating your carpets in the back garden twice a year was not sufficient to remove the germs and was anyway the physical effort was condemned by the *Lancet* as itself being injurious and dangerous to public health. What you needed was the Carpet Beating machine on display in Maynard and Cummings at 58 and 59 Seaside Road.

You could also find out more by attending lectures at the Devonshire Park Theatre by Mrs Longshore-Potts, a doctor of medicine who gave lectures on Health and Disease or Maternity for women only. All lectures were free although there would be a collection at the end. Each lecture would also be illustrated by 100 limelight views.

Of course there were not only medical doctors available. In 1879 there was J Howard of 14 Ashford Place who was a chimney doctor and sweep with many years experience.

Eastbourne Health – Drinking Water

Getting sufficient, good quality food for large families and with little family income was always a challenge but getting sufficient and safe drinking water was doubly important. Not only was it essential to be able to get enough water for hydration and the daily tasks requiring water such as cooking, laundry and bathing but drinking water had the added complication of being an extremely efficient vector for the many infectious diseases that confronted the Eastbourne public. The location of, usually, ground water and the high numbers of cess pools and other sources of infection was a problem throughout the world and, to a great extent as the publicity never failed to stress, Eastbourne was considered a leader in sanitation in terms of water provision and the removal of waste. Nevertheless Eastbourne folk were not immune to the risks involved in the collection of safe drinking water.

Prior to 1896 much of the water that the folk of Eastbourne used for drinking came either from streams or from wells drilled on their property but much of it was contaminated by human or animal waste. In 1869 a report said that water supplied from the Drove was wholly unsuitable for dietic purposes but the report was ignored. The water in question was derived from a well which stood nine feet from a former cess pool. This was also an issue in Old Town where the cesspits and privies of 1868 had generally been replaced by water closets but there was no water supply and, as a rule, the closets were placed outside the cottage doors causing a foul odour. The residents of Old Town obtained their water from the Motcombe Stream which had a pump installed close by the road side for people to access the water. The problem was that liquid filth and drainage from the farm flowed into the stream. The people then collected buckets of water and left them lying around their cottages ready for use. In 1896 the people of Old Town were banned by the Sanitary Committee from collecting water from the Bourne stream which they duly ignored with the result being 17 cases of enteric fever.

Meads was possibly even worse. In 1877 water taken from a well in Meads was declared bad as surface drainage from the land saturated with sewage had got into the water. Old Town and the eastern part of the town was also condemned to drink impure water in 1870 despite claims of high sanitation levels. Even the water from Bedford well was reported to be hard and salty and in 1895 there were complaints about the quality to the Council. The Eastbourne Medical Society passed a resolution stating that, in their opinion, the supply of water from the Water Company was unfit for drinking on account of the hardness and saltiness and that it was injurious to health. Despite representations being made by the Council to the Water Company to improve the quality they were ignored so the Council urged them to develop the water works at Wannock and Holywell. By 1896 the company had erected a large pumping engine at Holywell.

So the discovery of a pure and clean source of water in Holywell in 1896 was greeted with great fanfare and delight. Not only was this great news for the people of the town it was also advertised nationwide as a great benefit to the town and to the tourists. The *Lancet* reported the source of water as being palatable, wholesome and easily obtainable. Being a national publication it stated that there should be no reason why people should avoid Eastbourne which was one of the most sanitary towns on the south coast with such a very low a death rate. Nevertheless it was claimed that the discovery was not advertised enough citing the fact that Bovril was heavily advertised and so should Holywell water. As far back as 1871 it was suggested that anyone who drank Eastbourne water would beam with health over whoever dared to take a glass of Adam's ale elsewhere which would assuredly fill his unfortunate stomach with living organisms. Although the claims of good water back then might have been rather optimistic there seemed no doubt that the quality of the Holywell water was high. The chalybeate (natural spring water containing iron) spring was recommended to visitors as having the quality of the water found in the far famed springs of Clifton, Bristol. As regards stomach filling though there was a report in 1881 that a lady at a hotel had scolded her little boy because they had paid a high price for their dinner and the water he was drinking was filling him up.

Drinking even the clean, pure Holywell water might also be seen to be hazardous. In 1899 an inquest in Pevensey bay reported that the deceased had frequently drunk water in which she had a small amount of whisky. Of the latter she drank about a half a pint a day and although she had had some Bovril lately she had asked for water just before she died.

Of course finding the water was one thing but getting to the public was a different matter. Initially it was suggested that the street watering carts could be used to transport the water to central locations where people could collect their supplies. But, eventually, 100 men were employed to lay five miles of water mains to carry ten gallons of water a day for every resident to the east end in order that the working classes might find at their door the same supply which the better classes of residents and visitors enjoyed. Water might be a common factor but differences in status were to be preserved. The water was accessed through 40 to 50 stand pipes situated in different points in the town. One pipe at the junction of Enys Road lane and St Anne's Road showed the water flowing in a two foot tube to be fairly clear with a slight greenish tinge. It had 39.6 parts solid matter to 100,000 parts of water and contained no copper, lead or iron.

The availability of the water was trumpeted about the town. The New Hydro Hotel announced it was using it, brewers, mineral water manufacturers, pastry cooks, tea and coffee sellers were all using it and advertising the fact. It was indeed a big deal for the town and it looked forward to more wells being sunk in Friston and Wannock.

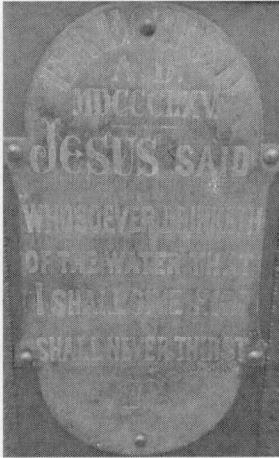

This drinking fountain was donated in September 1865
by Mrs. Elizabeth Curling (1790 - 1873), who lived
in Kent Lodge, Seaside Road (now Trinity Trees).
The fountain was originally located in the middle of the
road in Seaside, near the junction of Leaf Hall Road.
It was first moved to the corner with Langney Road,
probably in the 1950's before being restored
and relocated here on 21st December 2000.

Illustrations 8/9/10: Drinking water fountain now on Marine parade

Eastbourne Health – Hazards

Despite all of Eastbourne's natural advantages and it's carefully manufactured reputation as a premier health resort with an enviably low death rate, in health care terms, it could still be a hazardous place to live. As with the rest of the country the town's folk were always potentially exposed to the lethal infectious diseases for which there was no cure. There were also none of the medical or health care facilities available today and listed in the introduction to this book. Although there were few if any real 'cures' to the illnesses that could be suffered there were plenty of concoctions offered as treatments for huge ranges of disorders most of which were derived from organic sources and some of which were very keen to make plain that they contained no harmful or hazardous ingredients.

In 1890 Frazer's Sulphur tablets were confirmed to be free of mercury, arsenic and opium although it was never stated why anyone would want to incorporate such ingredients. In 1875 Crosby's Balsamic cough elixir which was widely advertised was declared free from opium. The Keating's cough lozenges of 1875 contained no opium, morphine or any violent drug. Dr Scott's 1891 Bilious and Liver pills were carefully prepared without the use of mercury. Wiseman's Infant's medicine in 1885 could be used for babies teething or if they were convulsed with wind or whooping cough because it did not contain laudanum (laudanum was a 10% solution of opium powder in alcohol containing opium alkaloids, morphine and codeine), poppies or opium. It was so popular that 1,656 bottles

104

of the medicine were sold in Gravesend in one year. Perhaps those taking the medicines were reassured that although they might not actually cure whatever they were being taken for they would not cause any more damage. Nevertheless despite some medicines being declared free of what might be considered extreme ingredients all of them were present in the everyday lives of Eastbourne folk both as medicines themselves or being present in non-health related areas that were not connected with the potential hazards they posed.

Arsenic

Perhaps the first association that is made with arsenic is its use in murders and there were, indeed many cases of murders caused by the administration of arsenic. In 1867 a survey of murders in Paris between 1851 and 1862 there were 232 murders using arsenic recorded, another 170 from phosphorus gained from matches, 30 using sulphuric acid, 6 using opium, 6 using hellebore (member of the butter cup family) and 1 using foxgloves (digitalis). Although arsenic was not always freely available it was fairly easily sourced with a gross of arsenic tablets being sold wholesale for 1/6d for a gross in 1889. In 1894 there was an inquest at the Six Bells in Chiddingly into the death of a man who was described as being steady but occasionally giving way to the drink for a day or two. He was noted as having bought a pound packet of arsenic from a Hailsham chemist allegedly for rat killing but he actually used it for his own suicide although the inquest found there was no evidence of insanity. In 1884 it was reported that a chemist had adopted a precautionary measure when selling arsenic. When asked by his drug clerk about selling a pound of arsenic to a person who would not reveal what he intended to use it for the proprietor stated that they should be careful about selling the arsenic so they should charge the buyer double the usual price. Although it was recognised that chemists would make a record of an arsenic buyers name and address in 1881 it was known that at the noisome emporia that were oil shops (hardware and ironmongers shops) it was possible to buy arsenic anonymously. But it was not necessarily the deliberate use of arsenic as a poison that could impact on the citizens. Arsenic could be found in many every day articles.

In 1889 arsenic was used in fly paper. However in 1884 the Liverpool police announced they were going to enforce the Sale of Poisons Act by taking proceedings against persons selling fly paper containing arsenic. This was after two women were hanged after being found guilty of poisoning a man using a solution of arsenic containing fly paper. Arsenic was also a popular rat poison but in 1876 dockers unloading a ship in Marseille were confronted with three large boa constrictors. To get rid of them they poisoned two pigeons with strychnine and fed them to the snakes two of which died. The third escaped. Perhaps poisoning three pigeons might have been a better plan but when the story was reported in England it was hoped such snakes would not be found in the London docks. Maybe snakes and strychnine would not be found in an Eastbourne garden but in 1896 the Royal Seed establishment in Southampton identified Paris Green which was an insecticide was 60%

arsenic, London Purple used 3-4 ounces of arsenic to 50 gallons of water and Gypsy Moth used 3 parts arsenate of soda to 7 parts lead. Deadly though the potions appeared to be to plants it might be presumed that the gardeners were also at high risk of using such chemicals. There was a case forwarded by a man in 1877 that the feeding of arsenic to horses would make their coats bright and that this was a common practice in the equine world. The fact that six of the ten horses he fed it to died might disprove this claim and the fine of £30 for killing the animals might make it less common practice.

If arsenic could be lethal to animals then so it could be for humans even if only through inadvertent exposure. In 1869 a Professor of Chemistry at the London Institute warned that the coal tar based dyes producing magenta, red and other brilliant colours were arsenical in origin and could be absorbed into the body from the 'showy' shirts the dyes were used in. If wearing a showy red shirt was not dangerous enough in 1862 it was said that a lady's ball dress which might be coloured green with arsenic would in one 'rattling waltz' throw off enough poison to kill a dozen people. It was hoped these dresses would soon go out of fashion or young men will abstain from choosing a partner wearing a poisonous dress.

In 1863 enamellers were cautioned about using arsenic in the manufacture of artificial flowers and that they should not be manufactured or worn at all because of the danger. By 1886 Cooke's of Leeds were advertising wall paper hangings that were all non-arsenical and not injurious compared with the previous hangings which did contain arsenic.

But arsenic was not always seen as a hazard. In 1895 the *Family Doctor* said that Dr Mackenzie's Arsenical toilet soap was one of the most economical beautifiers known to modern dermatology and would cause no irritation to even the most delicate skin. If the less than delicate skin around a hard corn was causing an issue then one could soak the foot in hot water and then pare down the corn with a knife ensuring there was no blood loss and then paint the corn two or three times a day with arsenic solution. If the corn was soft then the knife could be dispensed with and it could be painted with an arsenic solution until it dried up and disappeared.

It was also claimed that arsenic could actually promote health. In 1877 there were reports that in Styria, Austria arsenic was eaten for the purpose of developing personal beauty and increasing the strength of the body. In 1889 it was suggested arsenic could be used for skin conditions although it was acknowledged it did make people feeble and increased their heart action. It was also noted that chronic and acute arsenic poisoning had clear clinical symptoms. The effect of eating arsenic was to cause the eye lids to become sore, for the eye lashes to fall out and for the nostrils to become raw with the corners of the mouth cracking. It did not mention that death could be a by-product and it did not say if it mentioned this to the people of Styria.

Fatal though arsenic could be the Eastbourne Church of England Temperance Society were adamant in 1877 that the restrictions being put on the sale of strychnine and arsenic should be extended to the even more deadly poison alcohol.

Mercury

Another chemical that was, at the same time, recognised as harmful but also as a treatment was mercury. In 1868 Oakey's silver smiths soap used to clean and polish silver, plate glass and marble was considered safe to use as it did not contain mercury.

Other preparations that did contain mercury were highlighted as a risk. In 1881 the *Family Physician* advised that there had been a number of cases of injury from local mercury poisoning as it was used in the red India rubber frames used in the manufacture of false teeth. Mercury was used in the rubber to imitate the redness of the gums and make the plate seem more life-like. In 1884 Mr C S Ravenscroft of Hastings advised against what was considered the current vogue of covering the female face with wretched cosmetiques, powders, bismuths, lead and mercury which was plastered thicker and thicker on the face every day to hide the bad colour and stop up the cracks.

In 1876 Dr King advised that there were only two medicines that really acted upon the liver. One being the safe and acceptable Dandelion and Quinine and the other being mercury or the Blue Pill both of which had destroyed thousands of constitutions. Blue pills contained a high concentration of mercury and was used as a treatment for syphilis, TB, toothache and, especially on long ship voyages, for constipation. A more definitive denial of mercury came in 1898 from Dr G Stables in his book *Sickness and Health*. He claimed good and pure blood was made from wholesome food but never from physic. He accurately observed that medicines from unprincipled quacks would never cure anyone. Iodide of potassium was said to be largely used in the so called remedies but also used was the terrible drug mercury, arsenic and sometimes phosphorus and strychnine. Hazards potentially lurked in every 'cure'.

Opium

In 1864 the *Daily News* reported the presence of Chinese opium smokers in London. Although there were not a lot of reports of opium consumption in Eastbourne there was a lot of activity in the town concerning the drug. In 1880 the Eastbourne Anglo-Oriental Society held a meeting at the New Hall arguing for the suppression of the opium traffic. Until 1858 the profitable trade in opium between India and China had been run by the East India Company but after 1858 it was run by the Imperial Government and people in this country did not like it. The trade was very lucrative. In Bengal it was reported that in 1880 a crate of opium was worth £30 but when it was sold on in Calcutta it was worth £120. The effect being that the profit to the Indian Government was considered to be £3.5 million a year although some estimates put it at £13 million.

Whatever the commercial impacts the very presence of an opium trade incensed the people of Eastbourne who held many meetings to discuss and disapprove of the trade. In July 1880 the Society for the Suppression of the opium trade met in the New hall, Seaside Road. In 1883 the Committee of the Eastbourne Auxiliary of the Society for the Suppression of the opium trade invited all ministers to a meeting in the town hall in the January to call attention to the IMMORAL and DESTRUCTIVE CHARACTER of the TRADE. In 1892 an anti-opium meeting in the town called the opium trade Britain's National crime and in 1893 despite the inclement weather there was a well-attended meeting of the anti opium group at the town hall which passed unanimously a resolution condemning the morally indefensible opium trade.

Although opium was not in most medicines it was considered to be a good treatment for cholera. Masters of ships where a crew member suffered diarrhoea, possibly cholera, were advised to treat the man with an aromatic or astringent medicine containing a small amount of opium. Ten grains of the aromatic powder of chalk and opium were advised to be given in half a glass of peppermint water but if none was available five drops of laudanum would suffice.

Even on dry land in 1865 one case of cholera reported to be cured by administering five grains of opium and then one grain every half an hour. It was admitted one patient was hardly a scientific trail but it was claimed to work. Perhaps it was a less dangerous cure than that reported in 1867 from the *Cincinnati Journal* in the USA where a correspondent wrote that a case of cholera had been cured by injecting the patient with sulphuric acid.

Phosphorus

Perhaps not the most obvious dangerous chemical to be found in everyday life but there were murders committed using it as was shown in the Paris audit and there were areas where the public could be exposed to it in normal life. It was calculated that a small amount of yellow phosphorus, otherwise known as the 'Devil's Element' could be fatal although smaller doses could cause severe vomiting and diarrhoea that could be described as smoking when deposited. Phosphorus could be inhaled, ingested or absorbed through the skin.

Perhaps the best example of the danger of phosphorus were the Lucifer match girls working for Bryant and May. Their working conditions in 1862 were very bad working long hours for little pay and strict working conditions with no Health and Safety legislation to protect them. The Lucifer matches were well known as being cheap, commonplace and useful but they were also considered to be the cause of many fires. Their main health problem was that the phosphorus that was used in their manufacture caused a malady called 'necrosis' in the workers that made them. The vapours of the white phosphorus that was created when they were made caused the jaws of the factory girls to rot away with the lower jaw sometimes being completely eaten away. This became known as 'phossy jaw'. In addition to the bone rot the gums developed a greenish white glow that could be seen in the dark. This continued until 1906 when the use of phosphorus in matches was made illegal. Bryant and May also marketed a special safety match that were not poisonous and did not contain phosphorus.

It was not just the factory girls that were at risk. In 1899 it was reported that a child was killed by sucking matches containing phosphorus which was declared highly poisonous. The treatment was to give the patient barley water mixed with carbonate of magnesia after a good emetic. Under no circumstances should oil be administered.

Even in 1864 Letchford's were selling hygienic non-poisonous matches made without phosphorus, brimstone or any poisonous ingredients and were also free from smell.

But it was not all bad news for phosphorus. In 1878 Coleman's Phosphorus, Quinine and Pepsin pills could restore strength after overwork and anxiety with the phosphorus particularly soothing the brain. Freeman's Syrup of Phosphorus was the most wonderful blood purifier and nerve tonic brought to the public in 1885. One dose of it was claimed to be equal to ten doses of cod liver oil. Attenburrow's the chemist of 2 Compton Street, Devonshire Place stocked quinine, phosphorus and *nux vomica* pills which were claimed to be the best nerve tonic and brain restorative. *Nux Vomica* was actually an unsafe tree seed containing strychnine and brucine which were both toxic but it was claimed it was good for constipation, anxiety, migraine and many other conditions.

In 1866 the absence of phosphorus was considered by Dr Griscom to be the cause of tooth decay as well as scurvy, nervous diseases and insanity. He claimed there was fourteen times as much phosphorus in bran than in superfine flour so brown bread was fourteen times as nutritious.

In 1880 phosphorus was actually praised by M C S O'Kelly of the Gildridge Cigar store in 3 Terminus Road who said in a testimonial that Cobden's quinine and Phosphorus pills were simply marvellous. They were an invaluable stimulant and brain tonic that threw off the germs of disease producing cheerfulness, vitalising and enriching the blood as well as curing impotence, skin eruptions and melancholy.

Eastbourne Health – Hospitals

Acacia Villa

In 1891 the Sanitary Authority had the power to inspect, cleanse and disinfect houses and their contents including bedding and clothing which might have been exposed to infection and for the enforcement of penalties for hindering such operations.

In September of 1895 the Sanitary Authority provided, in accordance with the provisions of the Infectious Diseases Prevention Act of 1890 a house for the isolation of persons during disinfection of their house.

The house provided was Acacia Villa, 391 Seaside, later known as the Isolation Cottage, and it was used as a temporary home for residents who were having their houses fumigated after an infectious disease outbreak. It was opposite the Archery Recreation ground.

In its first year, 1896, it sheltered 30 people using the five rooms available but as the numbers of cases of infectious disease fell it was used less and by 1903 it had been used by only seven people.

With rent/rate and taxes being £35 3s 12d, Coal and water being £6 17s 6d and nursing £6 9s 0d it was quite an expensive asset although it was frequently praised by Dr Willoughby in his reports. It was let to the Eastbourne Corporation on a seven year lease from 29th September 1902 at an annual rent of £32.

Iron Hospital

The provision of a hospital that could accommodate and treat people with infectious diseases appeared to be a priority in the town. There was considered to be no need for a hospital to treat any and all other disorders as it was assumed that the medical men in the community could attend to all other illnesses and disorders that the population might suffer. One such infectious disease hospital, although intended to be functional for six months caused a deal of consternation in the town for a number of reasons.

In January 1877 the Eastbourne Local Board met to discuss the provision of a temporary infectious diseases hospital. The initial proposal to build on a strip of land above the Union was discounted as being too small so it was recommended that Montpelier House in Old Town was purchased for £2000 despite claims a hospital could be built elsewhere for £700. The Iron Hospital, when complete, would consist of just eight beds.

Of course there were objections particularly because it was claimed that the Ocklynge area was being covered in first class villas and residents would not want an infectious diseases hospital in their midst even if it were only for six months. But construction went ahead with a larch pole and rail fence with an oak gate surrounding the building – a well-known barrier to infection transfer. A receiver for the sewage was to be installed and in what seemed a rather late proposal the Water Company was to be asked to lay water on to the hospital.

By October the hospital had been completed and it quickly attracted much criticism. It was considered to be defective in construction and arrangements for its function. There were accusations that the building had started before plans had been submitted for approval. This might explain the lack of classification of sexes or diseases, no laundry, mortuary or disinfecting chamber.

Overall it was considered the money that had been wasted on the project would have been put to better use by building a proper cottage hospital.

In 1877 the Guardians of the Eastbourne Union were given permission to erect a hospital for pauper infections on the workhouse premises. In 1878 the Guardians put out a tender for the erection of an infectious disease hospital on the grounds of the work house.

Leaf Homeopathic Cottage Hospital

In 1903 Sir Henry Tyler the Chairman of the House Committee of the London Homeopathic Hospital said in a speech made at the Eastbourne Homeopathic Cottage Hospital that it was lamentable that those who knew of the 900 remedies that homoeopathists had investigated from animal, vegetable and mineral sources saw their friends and fellow-creatures suffering and dying when there were these remedies available.

In 1887 Dr Walther who, at the time lived in West House 1 Chiswick Place, was the local representative of homeopathy had proposed the establishment of a homeopathic hospital and, in response, the Misses Leaf who had an interest in homeopathy offered a small house, 2 Marine Road, in which to locate said hospital at a nominal rent. The site was described as being a secluded thoroughfare between the Royal Parade and Seaside and had easy access from the most populous quarters of the borough and situated in the heart of a very poor and populous district where the need for a hospital was painfully evident in a district as poor as the east end of Eastbourne.

In 1888 the house had been converted into a small hospital with four wards, eight beds and a child's cot and opened on January 2nd in the charge of 24 year old Caroline Emily Beavis from Clapham, London. In addition to Dr Walther who left the hospital in 1894 there was Dr A Croucher who worked at the hospital for many years and, at the time of opening, lived in Metford Lodge 17 Bolton Road. Both doctors were also intimately involved with the Homeopathic Convalescent Home in Enys Road.

Patients could be admitted to the hospital by letters of recommendation and no charge of any kind was made to patients with the supply of necessaries, medicines and advice being entirely gratuitous. A subscription of one guinea entitled the subscriber to place a patient in the hospital totally free of cost. It was noted that accidents could be received but only admitted on the production of a letter from a subscriber.

In the census of 1891 Miss Beavis, aged 28, was the head with the assistance of the lady nurse, Florence Coder and their servant Sarah Wood. At the time they had six patients including

Jane Morris who was 7 years old. By 1901 Josephine Foster was the assistant nurse and Emily Walls the servant with eight patients. By 1911 there was an additional night nurse, Camilla Hislop a cook, Clare Baker, servant Annie Harvey and Claire Tyler as well as 65 year old night watch Amelia Reynolds. Amongst their patients was Irene Pragnell who was five years old and described as an occasional patient.

The hospital proved popular and the newspapers reported the numbers of patients being discharged, admitted and resident each week. In one week in February 1892 7 patients had been discharged, 4 admitted and 1 remained in hospital. In August 1894, 9 had been discharged, two had died and none admitted or in residence. Also in 1894 it was claimed that 65% of in patients and nearly all out patients were cured during the year. But by 1903 number 2 Marine Road was considered to be too small for the workload and it was proposed that a new site be found to build a new hospital. Unfortunately the £300 required to start the project could not be found so the Misses Leaf offered the use of number 1 Marine Road, Leaf House, next door. So on the first of February the hospital closed to open again on the 6th April after a refit that cost £695.

The two houses were now "fitted up throughout to meet modern hospital practices and had been re-decorated presenting quite a cheerful appearance." Accommodation was extended to ten beds and a child's cot and the waiting room set aside for out patients to attend between 9.30 and 12. There was also a well fitted operating room with a parquet floor and excellent accommodation for the staff including the matron Miss Bevis who was to remain matron for 23 years dying in 1911 when the new matron Miss Bratten took over until 1913 when the matron was a Miss Tucker.

Technology was also incorporated in the development with an upgrade to the electric lights with electric bells being installed and telephonic communications between various parts of the institution. The bathroom was well lighted and had a fireplace. The walls of the wards were tinted with a green and white impermeable paint which was restful to the eye.

In the February of 1903 a Miss Annie Savage collected £52 11s 10d and amongst other things she bought "gas and ether apparatus" for the hospital.

By the time of the upgrade 2000 sufferers had been treated with only 30 having a fatal termination and it served over 50 medical practitioners in Eastbourne. In addition the committee appointed a night nurse to make the duties of Miss Bevis less arduous.

By 1914 a third house had been added, number 3 Marine Road, at a cost of £750 although "at that end of town they went on the principle that they would not start anything until they had the money". The hospital now had 14 beds, 2 children's cots and an X ray machine.

By 1915 there were sixteen beds although six were set aside for soldiers. By 1917 100 wounded soldiers had passed through the hospital. They also advertised that the hospital was open for visitors on Sundays, Tuesdays and Fridays between 2 and 4pm.

Of course being a charity the hospital was always seeking funds and there were endless events such as concerts, plays, reading and works of sale as well as donations, collections and help from Friendly societies but it was always a struggle.

In 1905 it was reported that several times during the past year the coffers were in a badly depleted state though by dint of several appeals the Treasurer just contrived to keep the wolf from the door. At the time the hospital had only a small share of the large, official Hospital Saturday and Sunday collections made in the town. In 1909 it was reported that it was an institution doing useful work but, financially, in low water.

In 1900 the valuable institution with 9 beds and a thoroughly efficient matron (Miss Bevis) was in urgent financial need and one gentleman had contributed £10 on condition that others would raise the total to £50. Amongst the many events in 1907 a Saturday evening was "Hospital Night" with a concert at Leaf Hall to proceeds in aid of "that deserving institution". By 1910 the Watch Committee gave their kind permission for the hospital to hold its first street collection on the 7th August when £92 11s 11d was collected. Hospital boxes had collected £22 0s 6d in the year.

Not all fund raising events went smoothly and in 1924 the proposed sale of work to be held at the Town Hall was found to clash with the unexpected Election Day. There was an appeal to the public to make time to come and support the sale and not to let their political activities prevent them from doing so.

Pound Days were particularly popular and attracted large donations of food and other commodities. Amongst others in 1915 43 lbs of Quaker Oats, 4 and a half lbs of matches and 79 lbs of tea were received.

Finances aside there were good times and in 1916 it was reported that the Yuletide spirit was manifest everywhere. The wards were cheerfully decorated and on Christmas Day the patients were regaled with a seasonable repast of the traditional nature.

In 1930 the Medical officer of Health, Dr Willoughby reported that the Leaf showed that the average number of beds unoccupied was over the 15% deemed acceptable. Perhaps the hospital was becoming less popular.

Although site development progressed over the 44 years by 1932 a new hospital site was being proposed claiming that "if the difficulties could be visualised under which this hospital is carrying on, the narrow passages, the inconvenient wards, the different floor levels in the converted houses which form the premises you would understand why we so urgently need new premises".

From January 1932 there was a relentless fund raising campaign to raise enough money for a new hospital. From the "£3500 (which the hospital has in hand) will enable building to start employing local labour. Another £13,000 would complete the scheme free of debt". Donations were requested by the Appeal Secretary who had a telephone number 148. By 1934 the sum required had reduced to £10,000 and, in encouragement, it was stated that the unemployed building trade would benefit enormously by the building of the hospital. Approximately 40% of the cost would be spent in wages and the contract would be given to a local firm.

In 1933 the Leaf Homeopathic Cottage Hospital moved to St Anne's Road with the foundation stone being laid in the October by John Slater MP and became just the Leaf Hospital. It too closed in 1974 with services moving to the new District General hospital. In 1983 it was re-opened as the Leaf Hospital, Department of Podiatry, University of Brighton.

In 1937 it was reported that there had been a loss of £1,156 on the sale of 1-3 Marine Road with the Charity Commission selling them for £2,200 against them being worth £500 each 47 years ago.

Illustration 11: Leaf Homeopathic Hospital Marine Road

Princess Alice Memorial Hospital

In 1874 the magnificence of the invalids whom fate and physicians had sent to the tepid foreshore of Eastbourne, a watering place which seemed to have been built for the upper hundred thousand of middle classes who congregate in and adorn the town was commented upon. Eastbourne always had aspirations of grandeur. In contrast to the magnificence it was suggested that the less pecunious classes to whom cold joints were familiar should put up with Thanet, Kent joys with appetites that, happily, the Thanet air can so bounteously offer. In other words if you have money welcome to Eastbourne, if you do not then Kent is for you.

But although Eastbourne was keen to be a convalescent centre for out of towners it was sadly lacking any hospital facilities for the resident population.

The fact that Eastbourne was becoming a larger town with up to 20,000 residents meant in the early 1880s that a hospital was much needed and it was proposed that the cost could be borne by the ratepayers of the town. Naturally, this being Eastbourne of course, there were plenty of arguments against having a hospital at all. In 1876 it was pointed out that there was no need for a hospital when there was the Union which had a hospital block. Even there only a couple of small pox cases had been reported at one time but a third nurse had been employed only to find she had nothing to do. The argument for the hospital was that one was needed in case of emergency. This was countered by suggesting the town should have its own army in case it was threatened with invasion. In almost a concession to the project it was suggested that land in Langney could be bought for £20 an acre but this was considered to be too far out of town for a hospital.

In 1879 a letter writer sent two letters pointing out that Eastbourne already had a military hospital, a convalescent hospital, an infectious diseases hospital and a hospital for the really poor with the County hospital but an hours ride away. Why would we need another? It was pointed out that the cottage hospital in Margate, a town three times the size of Eastbourne, averaged less than 2 people attending per day with 25 patients a year and all six beds being sometimes empty. Why should Eastbourne ratepayers pay so much for so little especially when it was claimed that "it is notorious there are relatively no poor in Eastbourne and the present medical staff in the town were equal to any emergency". Just as a counter to the lack of activity in a hospital there was a letter complaining that the writer had attended the London hospital with a man who had broken his arm. They had arrived at 8.35am and were not seen by a doctor until after 10am and the waiting area was full of people seeking treatment. The waiting time was unacceptable.

By 1877 there had been discussions about the provision of a general hospital in Eastbourne but the Local Government Board had not sanctioned such a project. Eventually the decision to erect a hospital was made in 1879. It was to be a suitable reminder of the late Grand Duchess of Hesse, Princess Alice of Great Britain and Ireland and it would be called the Princess Alice Memorial Hospital and would provide not less than 12 beds.

To get things going a committee of no less than 51 people was convened and the first task was to raise the £4000 needed for the building. The Eastbourne Provident Dispensary generously promised £900 later rising to £1000 but after a falling out nothing was actually contributed. Raising the rest proved difficult and by the August of the year they were still £2000 short. By 1881 the cost had risen to £4500 with £2300 still needed.

Undaunted, while still raising money for the project, tenders were put out for the building work and those received ranged from £6650 from Cornwell's in Eastbourne to £4357 from W Gregor in London and his tender was accepted but to keep costs down one wing of the planned hospital was dropped. Even ahead of the opening discussions were held to ensure that people who could pay for treatment could not access free services from the hospital and that everyone should pay something depending on their circumstances.

Once the principle of the hospital had been agreed, and as this was Eastbourne it took some time, the siting was the next issue. The Upperton area was favoured but in 1881 there were concerns that if that was to be location it might be too close to the railway lines and there would be too much noise from the continual running to and fro of the trains not to mention the smoke pollution and the shrieking whistling noises. Meads was considered to be a much better and quieter place for it but this was discounted as it was deemed too far for the doctors to travel to.

Eventually the principle and site were agreed but just as the foundation stone was being laid in 1882 it was noted that the Eastbourne Provident Dispensary planned to build a cottage hospital as well. It appeared that the two organisations were trying to out rival each other. There had been concerns in 1881 as to how the Princess Alice hospital would support itself and whether it should accept private, paying patients now with the prospect of a rival charitable hospital there would be double the charitable demands on the town folk trying to support two hospitals. The other view in 1883 was that with the Princess Alice, All saints Convalescent home, the Cottage Hospital not to mention the work house infirmary and the infectious diseases hospitals Eastbourne would have an excellent name for providing ways and means for the relief of pain and suffering. Ironically it was suggested that in such a remarkably healthy town as Eastbourne there was not the slightest need for two 'general' hospitals. The strain on pockets was exacerbated in 1885 when there was opposition to the proposed moving of the Jevington Convalescent and Invalid home to Eastbourne with the running costs being borne by the residents of the town. In 1890 an annual subscriber to the Princess Alice who donated £50 a year or £1000 as a life time donation could nominate 12 patients a year, free, for three weeks each. For half those sums they could nominate six patients a year.

In 1883 the building was complete and the Prince and Princess of Wales came to Eastbourne to open on the 18th June to open it. To accommodate 500 of the crowd a grand stand was erected directly opposite the entrance to the hospital with ticket prices of 10/- to 2s 6d. As part of the ceremony there was a presentation of purses containing no less than 5 guineas by young ladies of the town to His Royal highness the Prince of Wales.

At the first annual meeting of governors and subscribers held at the School Rooms in South Street it was observed that the first case was admitted to the hospital on the 1st July with 37 people being admitted in the following six months some cases being grave and serious accidents. With a degree of satisfaction it was reported that the hospital was always prepared for sudden emergencies with a spare bed and plenty of hot water. Modern hospitals are presumably just as well equipped for emergencies. They were also pleased to report that portraits of Queen Victoria, the late Prince Consort, the Prince of Princess of Wales and the late Princess Alice had been displayed on the walls of the building. The institution had been functioning well but there was concern that no clergy had called at the hospital or made any arrangements to attend the inmates (not referred to as patients) but it was hoped this would change as the newness of the institution wore off.

The hospital was kept quite busy. In 1885 215 patients attended, and by 1897 284 had been admitted with 20 attending out patient's clinics, 52 accident victims being seen and 26 major operations being conducted. The newspapers were pleased to report in great detail the people attending the hospitals, their diagnoses and treatments including operations they endured. Again, at the time there was no consideration of patient confidentiality!

The hospital was to be run through subscribers and charitable events but to raise money and, more importantly to distinguish it from the work house infirmary patients were charged for its services. In 1884 a Mr J H Campion Coles had to deny a report that poor persons were not admitted to the hospital except upon paying a large sum weekly. He stated that patients were charged according to their means with sixpence being the lowest daily charge. In 1885 there was a breakdown of the charges the 215 patients incurred:

- 4 paid 3 shillings (3/-) a day
- 45 paid 1 shilling a day
- 1 paid 10 pence (10d) a day
- 88 paid 6 pence a day

So popular was the hospital that it soon expanded from the original 12 beds that were planned. So busy were the extensions that in 1889 the Management Committee advertised for temporary accommodation in the town for patients during additions and alterations to the hospital. They would be glad to receive offers from owners of empty houses or buildings suitable for such a purpose.

In 1890 the committee reported 227 cases which was an increase of 38 on the previous year. Of these 119 had been cured, 44 had been relieved, 5 were unrelieved, 1 was considered unsuitable for treatment, 6 had been discharged on their request, 8 had died, 1 had been sent to the Sanatorium, 1 had been sent to the Union House and 23 were still in hospital and there had been 55 accidents treated. The average length of stay had been 27 days. But the principle event had been the erection of a children's wing with a small ward being called the Catherine Ward after Mrs Catherin Whelpton and the 7 bed children's ward being called the Geraldine after Mrs Wrangham. In total there was another 10 beds. By 1891 the children's wards were called the Alexandra wing but it was noted the building of it had put the hospital into debt.

But this did not stop development. In 1897 the plans were to provide an isolation ward, an outpatient room where waits could be attended and wounds dressed, a waiting room for admissions to the hospital, a room for the treatment of outdoors patients and a place for delirious patients on the isolation ward.

In 1899 £2500 was required for an extension possibly to be called the "Home Wing". It was also proposed that the new "Jubilee Wing" would give accommodation for 6 extra beds, a board room and a sitting room for nurses. On the first floor there would be 5 good bedrooms for the nurses. In addition the isolation ward would be built against the existing children's ward but cut off from the rest of the hospital. It would have three beds available for noisy patients and there would be improvements to the kitchen.

The hospital was closed in 1977, demolished and replaced with a commercial retirement home.

Illustration 12: Princess Alice Memorial Hospital

Princess Alice Memorial
Cottage Hospital
Eastbourne

Sanatorium

A sanatorium is defined as a place where a person afflicted with an illness could be cared for. In the early Victorian times this was primarily a place where patients with an infectious disease could be cared for, albeit with a paucity of effective medicines and treatments. The great scourges of the times were infectious diseases such as small pox, diphtheria and measles. Without effective treatment to limit spread the only two defences the pubic had against these diseases and others were prevention and the isolation of those who contracted the diseases.

Isolation could be achieved in a number of ways. Simply an affected person could be isolated in their own home despite this being difficult in an overcrowded house. The more affluent, especially those from out of town could, perhaps, rent rooms as was the case in 1876 when two unfurnished bedrooms for permanency, to be used as a sanatorium as required were advertised for. The large numbers of private schools in Eastbourne were all proud to advertise a sanatorium on their grounds. In 1878 Clifton House School which had been established in 1836 boasted a very pretty and inviting detached sanatorium but it had had no occupant except a small fox terrier dog who was exiled into it because of his unconquerable dislike of cats. Perhaps good news if parents were looking for a healthy school for their boys to attend especially as it would cost 40 guineas a year for boarders.

But for Eastbourne residents the sanatorium meant a larger institution that could accommodate patients with infectious diseases. Despite the fact that Eastbourne had been and remained unusually free of such difficult and threatening cases in 1875 Eastbourne boasted the first infectious diseases hospital.

In 1877 the Local Government Board sanctioned the erection of an infectious hospital in the grounds of the Union work house and this was duly erected but there were to be constant disputes as to whether the sanatorium should accept infectious patients from the work house and whether it should disinfect the clothing and linen used by infected souls in the work house.

It appeared a distinction had to be made between the sick destitute and others who better qualified for care in the sanatorium.

In 1878 the Lighting and Building Committee recommended plans for a new and separate sanatorium to be built in Old Town. Discussions were had regarding the site for the institution and as the previous infectious hospital had been at Bourne Hollow it was suggested that the new sanatorium should be on the south side of the Old Town cemetery. This was eventually turned down and the site in Upwick on the East Dean Road was selected. A lease on the land for 88 years for use as an infectious disease hospital was granted by Mr Carew Davies Gilbert in 1885. The Sanitary Committee after agreeing to borrow £5000 to cover the cost of the building then put out a tender for architects to design a Borough Sanatorium that would accommodate 40 patients with stalls for three horses. This, considering the favourable hygienic conditions of Eastbourne and the almost entire absence of fevers in the town was considered to be ample for ordinary requests. By 1886 a tender for the erection of the sanatorium was issued and those losing crops as the agricultural ground was turned over to a building site were compensated. In 1887 the Corporate Seal was affixed to the contract for George Hartfield to start excavating, levelling and preparing the ground for building.

As the building progressed there were complaints about the number of unforeseen bills that kept cropping up. One such was proffered by the Fire Brigade who inspected the site and recommended a new water main, fire hydrants, three 40 foot lengths of leather hose, six fire buckets and two hose spanners amongst other things at a cost of £90 12s. Other items were less costly with a request in 1892 for the donation of a piano for the use of inmates and the staff.

In 1888 the Corporation of Eastbourne advertised for a properly qualified medical officer and superintendent for the new borough Sanatorium. The pay was to be £50 a year and 10/6d a day for attendance on patients when there were more than one in the sanatorium under his care. In 1894 a porter to attend the disinfection and incinerator as well as providing general assistance was advertised for. For this, on the face of it risky post, the pay was to be 1 guinea a week with board and a certain degree of uniform. Possibly personal protective equipment (PPE) but unlikely to be so. By 1889 the sanatorium was up and running with an annual expenditure of £522 15s 4d.

Perhaps neither should have been particularly worried about contracting any diseases. In 1895 the presence of the sanatorium had enabled the citizens of Eastbourne to send infectious disease cases there with the effect that there had been a marked improvement in the health of the town. This seemed an odd conclusion as in June of the same year the sanatorium was declared completely empty with no cases requiring treatment. A distinct improvement on 1891 when there were 25 deaths. At the time the population of the town was put at 46,698. Things did not change because in 1895 E Hart (cook) and Nurse Scott were given notice to leave as there were so few patients. Nevertheless there were plans to increase the size of the establishment. £1000 was requested in 1892 to provide a covered walk way to connect the administration block with the north and east pavilions preventing the nursing staff from being exposed to inclement weather and for the erection of a room for the reception and discharge of patients, when they had them, and a porter's lodge. There was some discussion about the covered way and the potential for aerial communication of disease between the wards and other buildings. An alternative with a roof but open sides was put forward. In 1898 the medical officer had advised there should be 1 bed for every 1000 population. At the time there were 17 beds in the iron hospital and 20 in the sanatorium but the iron hospital was not considered suitable in the winter.

The sanatorium was later to become the Downside Hospital with 7 blocks and 62 beds. It was to be joined by the Gildredge Hospital close by in 1914 which specialised in tuberculosis cases. Both hospitals closed in 1974 and made way for more housing. The area known as Upwick and the top of Church Street was becoming a more acceptable area to live. Much development had been taking place later in the nineteenth century despite complaints that residents had to make their way past the Work house and its infirmary, the sanatorium and before 1894 the slaughterhouse. This was close to the sanatorium but was eventually condemned with the owner who claimed to have invested in the property being compensated.

Illustration 13: Part of the Sanatorium

Small Pox Hospital

In 1902 a row between small pox vaxers and antivaxers had one side stating that during the Franco-German war (1870-1871) the French, who eschewed vaccination, lost 23,400 men to small pox but the Germans who were pro-vaccination lost only 300 men to the disease. The other side claimed the numbers were incorrect and different living conditions and quality of vaccination explained any differences. Statistics were roundly condemned as fake news by both sides. Nevertheless small pox was an important and disfiguring if not deadly disease, amongst others.

As late as 1911 Ianthe Cavendish reported a conversation held with the Countess de Noailles, an English women who married a French aristocrat and lived in Hollywell Lodge close to All Saints Hospital, claimed that the countess claimed vaccination was against every law of nature and did more harm than small pox itself. The countess though was though thought of as something of an eccentric. It was said she had a cow kept under her bedroom and a shaft let air rise. This was considered beneficial to health. She also enjoyed going to sea in a small canoe even when the sea was rough.

Also in 1902 the Eastbourne Medical Officer, Mr Hugh Stott, stated that of the 55 cases of infectious disease notified in the town 36 cases were diphtheria, 28 cases being in Hailsham with 24 of those being children under the age of 6. He suggested it was unfortunate that children under the age of six were compelled to attend school as they spread the diseases. The implication being that they should self-isolate at home. Mr Stott said that those that had not had the small pox vaccination should be fined or vaccinated without delay.

The previous year the Hailsham Small Pox Emergency committee reported they were in negotiations with the Eastbourne Town Council for the use of the Corporation Small Pox Hospital at Langney when required.

In 1855 there was granted a site at Old Town on which to erect a hospital at a small sum per annum with no limit as long as it was used for the purpose of a hospital. The nominal rate was 5/- per acre for as long as it was used as an infectious hospital.

By 1877 the Hospital Committee had the choice of three sites to build an infectious hospital; the Ordnance yard which was considered impractical, an iron building in some unidentified, isolated spot on the Crumbles or the purchase of Montpelier house an isolated detached house in Old Town a short distance from the road with a half an acre of ground although it was considered unsuitable as there was no means for proper isolation of smallpox and there was anywhere to convert into a mortuary.

In his annual report of 1894 for the Borough Isolation Sanatorium (infectious hospital) in Upwick the Medical Officer Dr W.G.Willoughby stated that there had been 91 patients admitted with infection disease with 7 deaths (mortality rate 7.7%). This was in comparison with 91 admissions in 1889 with 29 deaths (mortality rate 31.8% and 271 admissions with 59 deaths (mortality rate of 21.7%). It was noted that the great majority of patients were under the age of fifteen with, mainly, scarlet fever then diphtheria, which was more fatal, and enteric fever. Being young was a dangerous period of life at the time. In the ten years prior to 1861 it was reported that there had been 787 deaths in Eastbourne. Of these 154 (20%) were children under the age of 10. The average length of stay in the sanatorium was 54 days with scarlet fever and 20.5 days for diphtheria with stay being 16 days for fatal cases.

Some of the costs were listed as:

Keep: £735 4s 6d
Drugs: £63 3s 5d

Horse Hire: £33 5s 3d
Forage: £40 6s 10d

The average cost per patient was £16 8s 3d including disinfection.

There was a matron, three staff nurses, 4 assistant nurses, 2 ward servants, 3 house servants, 2 laundresses and 2 men (a groom and a disinfector/ porter).

In response to the town having 15 cases of small pox and two deaths in 1895 the Langney Hospital, one of three infectious disease hospitals in the town, was built on land that belonged to the Duke of Devonshire and was considered far enough away from Eastbourne to be safe, for £1250. Previously small pox cases had been treated in the Iron Building at the Sanatorium.

Erected in the October it was in use in the November. It was an 18 bed, 4 ward single storey corrugated iron building on the Crumbles very close to the water front with a small wall around the property site. The site, despite the wall was in an area which led to its ultimate closure in 1940 and demolition after the war partly due to the encroaching sea. It was not a busy hospital. In 1912 two cases were isolated there and in 1900 an advertisement in the Eastbourne Gazette gave an indication of the throughput. The advertisement for Langney Hospital was for a man and woman to act as caretaker of the Borough Hospital for small pox at Langney. It stated the hospital was rarely used so duties were generally simply cleaning and caretaking although the wife must be able to cook and do laundry. The salary was to be £1 1s 0d per week, cottage and fuel etc. included.

Despite the lack of patients in 1902/3 the expenses of the hospital were £84 12s 6d but the receipts were only £5 5s 0d putting a strain on the council budget.

Initially the hospital had two nurses as well as the man and his wife acting as caretaker and servant but this was reduced to one nurse. In 1896 there were 149 people admitted to the Sanatorium but only one to the Langney Hospital and this was frequently repeated with no patients at all being admitted 1n 1898 or 1899 and two in 1900 with none in 1904/05/06. A burst of activity in 1902 had four patients. One a tramp from Gravesend, a resident of Eastbourne who had visited London and the caretaker and his wife who had refused vaccination.

By 1902 the Sanatorium had been extended and was "now of a size and extent adequate for the special needs of a health resort and school centre such as Eastbourne". It now had 6 pavilions, 65 beds and electric lighting. The Eastbourne Schoolmasters Association and later in 1904 the Eastbourne Schoolmistresses Association retained by paying £150 and £180 per year exclusivity of pavilions which were now named which did away with the necessity of large schools adding a local sanatorium.

In 1904 the Railway Passengers Assurance Company offered Employer Liability insurance for Accident or Disease (Small pox, scarlet fever, diphtheria or appendicitis). The agent being Mr T W Dean with offices in the Railway Station, Eastbourne.

By 1928 the Medical Officer's report noted that it was particularly gratifying to find Eastbourne had maintained its reputation as a health resort so far as infectious diseases were concerned. No cases of small pox had been reported and this was a source of great satisfaction.

But in 1929 the hospital was briefly opened for a small pox case.

The hospital was finally closed in 1940 due to encroachment of the sea and the town planners looking to develop the Crumbles for housing.

St Luke' Children's Hospital

The All Saints and Children's hospital in Meads was first established and in 1894 *The Hospital* said that, at the time, it was one of the oldest and largest institutions in the world with 500 beds, 100 of which were for children.

A meeting in 1888 was held at Devonshire House in London to discuss a scheme to build a children's convalescent hospital in Eastbourne and it was unanimously accepted. It would be associated with the All Saints Convalescence Hospital in Meads and would replace the totally inadequate small cottage that accommodated up to 40 children at the Home at Eastbourne. It would be a memorial to Harriet Brownlow-Byron the mother and foundress of All Saints, Margaret Street, London.

It was proposed that the 130 bed building should be three blocks of buildings on three floors in the Pavilion style located in front of All Saints Hospital. The ground and first floor of the three blocks would be connected by covered corridors wide enough for the children to play in. The top floor would have an isolation ward and there would be lifts to all floors. The cooking and warming would be done entirely by steam. The cost of the build was estimated to be around £10000.

The foundation stone laid by the Duchess of Albany in 1888. She had arrived in Eastbourne for the occasion on a special train that had left London Victoria at 10am and after stopping to pick up the Duchess it arrived in Eastbourne a few minutes before noon.

Her carriage from the station passed through highly decorated streets of Eastbourne. All the shops and houses along the road had bunting, flags and other decorations and as the carriage arrived at the hospital Mr Teeling's Juvenile Naval Brigade formed a guard of honour.

The hospital was eventually opened 1891 by the Prince of Wales (Later King Edward VII) but unlike the Duchess's visit there were no organised means proposed for decorating the town but an enterprising W Parks of 82 Terminus Road offered his services for public or private decoration for the visit of their Royal Highnesses. Anticipating a busy time he advised early applications were solicited to prevent disappointment. However the *Ladies Pictorial* reported that "a bright sky, a laughing sea, verdant with foliage, fluttering flags and smiling faces combined to welcome their highnesses".

On his arrival in the town the Sussex Artillery Volunteers Position Battery were to fire a Royal Salute and, at the hospital, the 1st Sussex Engineer Volunteers were to form a guard of honour. The *Ladies Pictorial* reported that "the Princess, who also opened the newly built children's wing at the Princess Alice Hospital, wore a beautiful costume of French grey silk entirely covered with exquisite lace and a dainty little bonnet with pink roses"

The building itself was of red bricks with blue banding and red roof tiles. There were three commodious and pleasant, airy day rooms and on each side an area was set aside for cripples. The low windows provided a fine view and there was a covered playground for wet weather but in good weather there were games of all descriptions and both day and night rooms had plenty of pictures and prints on the walls. The entrance was ornamented with sculptured figures and with the devices of a rose, shamrock, leek and thistle indicating it was open to sufferers from all parts of the UK.

It had 130 beds and the "vitiated air" was extracted by a foul air trunk running through the roof with flues opening into the same from every room and terminating in the kitchen flue which, being in daily use, made the extracting power automatic.

In the year the hospital had 42 girls and 10 boys in residence with supervision vested in the Sister Superior of the Convalescent hospital with the children being lovingly cared for by a number of sisters of the Community of All Saints,

Union Workhouse Infirmary

In 1794 in response to the threat of invasion by Emperor Napoleon a military barracks with accompanying stables was built on the site of what was to become in 1834, the Eastbourne Workhouse. With the invasion not materialising the buildings became surplus to requirements and the Eastbourne Guardians took them over and established the poor work house. Initially there was no separate provision for an infirmary with the well and sick being housed in the same spaces. As if that were not bad enough the 'nurses' looking after those that fell sick were the paupers themselves none of whom had any medical or nursing training at all.

Needless to say the work house had a dreadful reputation which was retained for many decades and, probably, for good reason. But by 1867 it was proposed that the sick poor in the Work house should be separated from the able bodied so that the name of the work house infirmary should cease to drive the destitute to the extremes of despair. A sentiment that reflected the view that the towns folk of any town had of their local work house.

In spite of the reputation the Union Infirmary had historically been viewed as being the general hospital of the town, in fact the only hospital of the town, and in 1877 an infirmary specifically for infectious disease cases was built on the site and this was to become the recognised infirmary from 1887 after being converted at a cost of £6100 with the work attracting 11 tenders. In addition to the conversion the Guardians purchased more land adjoining the infectious hospital site which was quite small.

The new infirmary was to have an east wing to accommodate old men and apartments for married couples, a west wing for epileptics and imbeciles and a new wing for 40 patients. Epilepsy was considered to be more a mental disorder at this time and there would be complaints that when mental asylums became fashionable they would be disproportionately filled with epileptics.

In 1889 the new building was considered to be a depressing and cheerless place with no pictures to relieve the coldness of the surroundings and an appeal was put out for donations. In 1891 £325 was borrowed to install a new system of heating as not only was it was depressing but it was draughty and unhealthy.

Even one area where there might be considered to be some degree of luxury was cut back. Many of the cases admitted to the infirmary from outside its walls were serious and it was considered, medically, that the patients needed spirits and wine for their treatment. In 1884 the cost of alcohol used had gone down because the medical officer had reduced the consumption of porter from one pint to half a pint and even that was only allowed on his order. In comparison with other institutions it was considered the overall consumption of alcoholic liquors in the union was not excessive or unreasonable and in no way was it considered to be detrimental to the health of the inmates.

As well as being vilified for cutting the alcohol intake the visiting medical officer did not have an easy time. He was paid £100 a year but was expected to deal with a very wide range of patients. In 1888 the Guardians considered the issue of the medical officer having to pay for all the medicines he used out of his own pocket. Miss Brodie Hall advocated that the medicines, which were estimated to be worth £20 a year should be paid for by the board and not the medical officer. The Guardians considered that if he did not have to pay then his salary could be reduced to £90 a year. Eventually it was suggested the Board paid for everything and his salary should remain the same but as he could not be bothered to turn up at the meeting discussing the issue the whole subject would be carried over. Therefore in 1889 the *Hospital* pointed out that the medical officer in Eastbourne was still paying for medicine and appliances out of his own pocket an arrangement that could lead to the temptation of providing inferior medicines. Quite what the definition of an inferior medicine when virtually none of them worked at all was not explained. In any event this was something that the Eastbourne MO Mr Farnell was considered unlikely to do as he was considered an excellent doctor who visited the infirmary two or three times a day and would rather earn nothing than skimp on medicines or appliances.

As well as improvements to the accommodation there were starting to be improvements in the nursing care by actually employing nurses who knew what they were doing. A Miss Wilhelmina Brodie Hall, a female Guardian was instrumental in bringing in nurses who had been trained and were supplied through the Workhouse Nursing Association. However in 1890 the Local Board was under the impression that the infirmary was no longer recruiting through the Association despite the fact that the present head nurse had been recruited through that route and was considered the best nurse they had ever had.

The problem was that any thoroughly trained nurse would rather go to work in a large hospital in preference to working in a work house infirmary. It was noted in 1890 that when the Board advertised for a nurse they had applicants who called themselves nurses but were not trained and had only picked up the little knowledge they had through working with others. It was claimed they were not nurses in the scientific meaning of the word.

To try to remedy the situation in 1886 the Local Government Board consented to the Guardians subscribing £2 2s per annum to the funds of the Association for Training Nurses for Workhouse Infirmaries. In 1894 the indominatable Miss Brodie Hall not only improved the nursing arrangements at the infirmary and did great works looking after the town orphans but also advocated the appointment of an efficient cook and secured the boon of treacle with the patient's rice pudding.

In 1889 the Guardians decided to build a new infirmary. It was to be of plain red brick and two storeys in height. It would occupy 3 acres and 2 roods (a quarter of an acre or 40 square perches) and be 316 feet long with an administration block separating the male and female wards. There would be 108 beds with a special provision for children, lying in (maternity) cases and isolation cases. The epileptic hospital would have 9 beds. The 4 wards were to be heated with ventilating stoves and the smaller wards by ventilating grates. The whole would cost £6100.

In 1898 there was a suggestion that the old Epileptic hospital which had been set apart for the use of married couples be used for children under the age of three. It was pointed out that there was only one married couple at present and in the previous ten years only one married couple had expressed a wish to live together.

To raise funds for the infirmary in 1898 there was a sale of articles made by aged inmates of the infirmary under the auspices of the Brabazon Employment Society who encouraged the infirm, sick and aged in work house infirmaries to make objects such as mats, rugs, baskets and woollen clothes to raise funds. Healthy inmates were not allowed to take part. The Brabazon project was initiated by the Countess of Meath in 1882 and was run locally by a ladies committee. By 1900 177 Poor Law unions were taking part as it was seen as a good way to raise funds.

The work house eventually became St Mary's Hospital which, in turn, was closed down and demolished making way for housing in 1990.

Furniture Hospital

If you had an urgent or special accident with your furniture at home you could engage the Furniture Hospital, the only one and oldest established one in Eastbourne. James Moorton at 103 and 104 Langney Road could assist without a letter at any time.

Eastbourne Health – Hygiene

Quite how the ordinary folk of Eastbourne or any town in the country felt about personal hygiene is difficult to judge as cleanliness and personal hygiene as we would measure it were difficult matters in the Victorian era. Bathrooms in houses were a rarity with most folk either having to wash in a galvanised bath tub that was brought out on occasion or not to bath at all. The mechanics of bathing were also difficult. Houses may not have had running water let alone running hot water so any water used had to be fetched from the shared well or pump or stream a bucket at a time. It then had to be heated on the range or over an open fire before being poured into the tin bath that already contained some cold water. Families usually used the same bath water for all members. Perhaps topping up with warm water along the way, with father going first, mother and then the children, of which there could be many, with the youngest going last and this may be, at best, once a week or much less frequently so there was a place for public baths where hot water was available on demand. Of course there was controversy over these as it was suggested that either people could wash in the sea or if they had not bothered to wash now why start now? Washing in the sea on a December night was not popular and, perhaps, 'Cleanliness being next to Godliness' was catching on.

Laundering clothes was also a very time consuming, laborious and difficult job requiring considerable physical effort. Clothes were soaked in water, scrubbed with soap agitated with a dolly and tub or rubbed across a wash board and then dried by passing them through a mangle or hanging outside to dry. As a result clothes were not cleaned as often as they are today but they still had to be cleaned at some stage so commercial laundries and even public laundries were set up. Proving it was a different age they offered that for the sum of one and a halfpenny the house mother may have at her command all the apparatus for the necessary but arduous process of washing. No washing, drying or ironing needed to be done at home and absolute privacy was secured for each worker. In addition they were popular meeting places. It was assumed no men would be using the facilities.

The issue of hygiene in a town that sold itself on its healthy atmosphere and conducive convalescent facilities was important. As early as 1867 it was understood that the welfare of the place depended very much on the hygiene measures being thoroughly carried out. In 1883 the proprietor of the *Eastbourne Gazette* was praised for providing, amongst other things, medical reports on the hygienic advantages of the locality which were distributed country wide. At the time there was a contrast between when the village of Brightelmstone, which was transformed into Brighton by the attendance of the Prince Regent, and its subsequent development with little knowledge of the science of hygiene and the advantages that Eastbourne had in its town design many years later.

In 1884 40 views of the principal places of interest in Eastbourne were sent to the International Hygiene Exhibition confident that visitors to the exhibition would desire to know in which town in England the science of hygiene was most situated. There could be but one answer to the enquirers and that town would be Eastbourne.

If townsfolk were ignorant of the science of hygiene there were many opportunities for education. In 1883 Dr Colgate gave lectures to ladies at the St John Ambulance Association on Home Nursing and Hygiene. In 1891 *Hygiene Medicine* offered pamphlets on Rheumatism for 7 stamps, on Consumption for 7 stamps and three pamphlets on young men for 13 stamps. In 1893 Dr Mary J Hall gave Medical and Hygiene lectures to ladies at the Town Hall. The lectures were free with a silver collection at the end or reserved seats at a shilling each. The Parks Museum of Hygiene opened at the University College to promote sanitary science. Montpelier House in Ocklynge Avenue offered courses of instruction in the Management of House Affairs and practical demonstrations of invalid cooking and hygiene. The British Viavi company offered ladies a series of drawing room lectures on Health and Hygiene at the Town Hall.

If there was nothing more to learn and the bathing and laundry situation was under control there were plenty of other opportunities to observe hygienic practices. In 1887 Miss Eva Chreiman offered hygienic physical training on her visits to Eastbourne where she would demonstrate the practice of Scientific Exercises - hygienically. The Upperton Steam laundry in Commercial Road near the Railway station offered hygienic laundering around 1893. The Electric Lighting Company as well as reducing its charges in 1896 advocated on behalf of the hygienic advantages of electric lighting over gas lighting.

In 1896 anaemia was reportedly sometimes found in people of advancing years who had neglected the laws of hygiene and were confined to badly ventilated sleeping and working rooms. They could do no better than take advantage of the tramway to convey working men to such a distance from town that they could obtain cottages preventing over-crowding and placing them under more favourable hygienic conditions. Of course Eastbourne did not have a tramway but it did have omnibuses and the town was expanding. The design of the west end of the town also prevented over-crowding and poor housing but this was not the case for the east end when in 1887 there was a call for the end of jerry built houses and a standard imposed to ensure the removal of the 'coffin dwellings' from the category of evils.

There were foods that could help the health of the population not least because they were produced hygienically. Gilbert's Prized Medal Bread was produced in 51 Seaside Road with hygienic machinery as was Hurst's noted white bread which was produced in the hygienic bread factory for a company that had been established for over 100 years. Presumably the implication being that all the other bakers worked in sewer like conditions. Letchford's Hygienic non-injurious matches which were made without phosphorus, any poisonous ingredient or Brimstone were available in 1864 and free from smell. Lighting a fire with a safety match to toast your hygienic bread was a major step towards the preservation of health.

If you needed something that would destroy and remove all active causes of disease from the system and achieve a permanent cure then you would need William Radam's Microbe Killer. This won a gold medal at the 1898 Hygiene Exposition in Paris as it was assimilated by all parts of the human frame as a health producing and nourishing element. Whether it was as nourishing as Van Houten's Cocoa which contained maximum flesh forming substances and was acknowledged by the medical profession is not recorded.

One of the more curious areas that promoted hygiene was the clothing industry especially the shoe sellers. In 1889 the Compton Boot and Shoe establishment in 46 Grove Road claimed to be specialists in hygienic boots and shoes. Indeed they advertised very heavily for decades but they did have competition. George Thomas Cripp ran the hygienic boot and shoe warehouse in 118 Terminus Road (near the new railway station) and in 1895 Vine's boots offered hygienic shapes from 9,11,13 Terminus Road.

But it was not just shoes. In 1890 the *Health* magazine recommended Reast's Invigorating Corset which could be purchased at Plummer and Lawford in 66a, 68 and 70 Terminus Road. It was thoroughly hygienic in nature and was made especially to correct round shoulders and stooping.

Perhaps somewhat more disturbing was the claim from George Brown and Company in Regent House, Eastbourne that, across the country, 80,000,000 lbs of old rags were ground up annually and mixed with wool to manufacture clothes. The concern was that the rags, in many cases, were not adequately disinfected before being re-cycled. This was not the case with his clothes which were sanitary and hygienic tweeds. They were made of a porous material which admitted a free circulation of air to the body and had the property of breaking up the malodours of the body into atmospheric gases.

If you preferred to make your own clothes then Madame Lowther Knights, the Principal of the Royal Counties Dressmaking College in Reading, demonstrated the European Hygienic system of dress cutting in the Town Hall in 1896.

As late as 1920 the Sussex Guide books said of Eastbourne that one of the outstanding features of the town was the cleanliness. Even in the poorest parts of the borough there was an absence of squalor in which respect Eastbourne was considerably in advance of many watering places.

Eastbourne Health – Hypnotism

Eastbourne worked hard on its image as a premier health resort and as well as the bracing air, leafy walks and sea there were numerous other areas of health care provision and Eastbourne was not slow to jump on any passing band wagon. Hypnosis was one such band wagon and it almost literally arrived in Eastbourne on a wagon. In 1895 Miss Ada Alexandra's great American circus arrived in town setting up in Simmons field, Seaside. As well as the normal features of a circus it boasted a leading feature being an exhibition of the hypnotic power of Professor Morris (there was a profusion of professors and European hypnotists) who was from the Royal Aquarium, Westminster (this was also closely associated with Professor Cooke who formed the Phrenological institute, another band wagon along with palmists, in Eastbourne in 1914). The professor would put a man into a death like trance in the circus in the morning and restore him in the evening.

This experiment was decidedly lower in class than the one performed by Professor Burko in the same year. The professor put 24 year old John Mills in a trance at London Bridge station and brought him down to Eastbourne on the 3pm train in the trance. Curiously Mr Mills had been put into a trance at the London Aquarium and stayed in the trance for 9 nights and 10 days. This event caused a great deal of concern and a question was raised about the legality and ethics of such an exercise with the Home Secretary. It was claimed that the plan was to keep the man in a trance for 30 days and it was viewed that this would be harmful to the man. The response was that the man was a free agent and had taken part in the experiment under his own consent and there appeared to be nothing harmful about the hypnosis. So John Mills was transported to Eastbourne lying in a casket eighteen inches wide with his body, with the exception of his face, covered with decorated cloth. He was then transported to the Pier Pavilion on a two horse wagonette with a band playing and men with flags acting as a cordon. When he arrived he was placed in the hall and scientific and medical men were invited in free of charge to examine him. Before 9.30 when the professor was going to wake the man several persons, some of whom said they were doctors, had examined him and despite the professor's invitation to try to wake the man none were able to rouse him. Of those who did examine the man only one felt it was a perfect sham to which the professor offered anyone £50 if they could undergo the same attention the hypnotised man had without reacting.

But this was not the end to the professor's exhibition in Eastbourne. In his farewell concert in the New Hall he selected two people for hypnosis claiming that any more would weaken the hypnotist but during his stay in Eastbourne he had hypnotised 46 people and three animals. There was no information about which animals were hypnotised, why they were hypnotised and how they could tell they were hypnotised. At the concert a Mr Beecham was also to give a lecture on hypnotism but had been unwell and unable to do so. Professor Burko claimed that Mr Beecham who would deliver the lecture was considerably superior to himself and was able to put a person into the sixth stage of hypnosis and to put anyone in the third stage if the abided by the rules and regulations of hypnotism without explaining what the stages or the rules were.

At the time there was no shortage of people offering to demonstrate the power of hypnotism. In 1889 Herr Carl Hansen the World Renown Hypnotist originally from Denmark but now direct from the Crystal Palace and Egyptian Hall to the Theatre Royal was to hold a hypnotic séance at 40 Grove Road. He was described as being a spectacle wearing 55 year old man, slightly below middle height with dark hair, beard and moustache. He described hypnotism or mesmerism as a nervous force proceeding from the eyes and tips of the fingers and was a great cure for nervous diseases. In an interview with a reporter at 30 Eastbourne Terrace Herr Hansen, who had married an English woman, said that he used to hypnotise his playmates when he was a child and the mesmeric power had been transmitted from father to son and he came from a hypnotic family. He did not mention if he was a lonely child or what any birthday parties must have been like if he kept hypnotising his friends. In agreement with Professor Burko he claimed hypnosis was exhausting and he could only manage eight to ten people a day.

His exhibition in Eastbourne was to consist of three hypnotic séances and illustrated lectures which would be of high scientific interest. The experiments were advertised as being exceedingly amusing and divested of all vulgarity and of such as will suit the most refined tastes. It was admitted that even if the experiments were of no practical value they would be exceedingly agreeable drawing room entertainment.

In 1891 a Mr Charles Rutland described as being a tall, handsome man with a deep voice had a large attentive audience at his demonstration of hypnotism at Devonshire Park Pavilion. With a slight degree of scepticism creeping in it was observed that his demonstrations might have been more believable if he had not used his colleague, W G King as his stooge. King was described as an actor (which might have come in useful) a humourist and thought reader. Nevertheless one of the demonstrations involved the insertion of a long needle through Mr King's arm and pricking him under the finger nail without him showing any effects and not even bleeding. It might have had no effect on Mr King but it was noted that several of the audience became so affected they had to leave the room.

In 1893 another German was advertising marvellous demonstrations of hypnotism illustrated by striking experiments. Herr Siegismund Kuehne offered to share the secrets of mesmerism, the mysteries of spiritualism and the wonders of hypnotism at the Pier pavilion with seats at 6d, 3d, or 1d. Despite only being 1d a seat the genuineness of the performance was questioned by a considerable section of the audience and, it was reported, there threatened to be something of an *emeute* (riot). This was not helped by the remarks made to the audience by Herr Kuehne.

Just to slightly demean the standing of the "scientific" hypnotism Mr and Mrs Victor Andre were offering marvellous entertainment at the Pavilion, Devonshire Park in 1895. They would demonstrate hypnotic clairvoyance supported by ventriloquial and musical performances and astounding feats of legerdemain (conjuring tricks).

Whether people were opportunists taking advantage of the latest craze is debatable but there was a pertinent observation in 1889. It was suggested that one day you were a nobody, nobody knew who you were or wanted to know you but the next day there was an article in an influential paper about you or something you have done. Suddenly everybody wanted to know you and they swarmed to your study or drawing room. This was the case for the Reverend Arthur Tooth who was a very amateur hypnotist who performed very ordinary experiments like getting a boy to sit and stand on command which, it was claimed, any teacher could do. Just as suddenly as he rose to hypnotic fame he was dropped returning to obscurity. One of his less than useful suggestions was that if hypnotism did not work then the patient should try self-suggestion convincing themselves that whatever was affecting them was now cured. Helpfully if this did not work the only person to blame would be the patient themselves.

But if hypnotism was a dubious entertainment was there any medical value in the system? In 1887 a Dr Berillon who was a well-known hypnosis specialist said it was impossible to overrate the value of hypnotic suggestions as a means of combating the objectionable habits which children were apt to contract. Forget the cure of cholera or small pox the doctor was more interested in stopping children from sucking their thumb and claimed it could be stopped with a single hypnotic session. Other treatments acted like magic and prevented relapse in kleptomaniacs.

Sufferers from sleeplessness in 1889 were advised that in hospital the best hypnotic was used especially for those engaged in brain work. Quite how the treatment qualified as a hypnotic is not stated but it entailed sponging the body all over with cold water just before going to bed. The sudden chill of the wash followed by the warmth of the bed clothes relaxed the congested condition of the vessels of the brain thus inducing sleep.

A more caustic assessment came from a Dr Richardson who called hypnotism a "fashionable epidemic" and asked if hypnotism could banish pain would the abolition of the pain be legitimate and long lasting? Would hypnotism dislodge chloroform as an anaesthetic? The answer was decidedly negative. His conclusion was that hypnotism was like other so called spiritual manifestations and would have its day and then cease to be.

Eastbourne Health - Infectious Diseases

The reign of Queen Victoria saw huge population demographic changes. People, in large numbers, started moving from the countryside where they supported a largely agrarian economy into the growing towns and cities where they took advantage of the better pay in the rapidly growing industrial economy. Although the wages in the cities were higher it could be argued that the living conditions were significantly worse. The housing was often poor quality, cramped, and concentrated into restricted areas and without proper water supplies or sanitation. Large Victorian families were crowded into a small number of rooms with several families all sharing a single house with little consideration for hygiene. This was a recipe for the spread of the bacteria that caused infectious diseases. Cesspools, inadequate or no drainage, drinking water being in contact with raw sewage and large amounts of sewage in the streets or spread over open areas were ideal breeding grounds for vectors of disease. The lack of knowledge about bacteria and the ways that infectious diseases were spread was a significant handicap to the containment of the spread of the often highly contagious disease and, of course, with no knowledge of the causes of the diseases there was no effective treatment although there were innumerable quack medicines and theories available – all completely ineffective. It is with this background that there were waves of infectious disease outbreaks around the country over the years with the large cities like London and Liverpool being the most affected but even smaller towns with many natural health related advantages such as Eastbourne were not totally immune and the town frequently had outbreaks recording numbers of deaths from diseases that are now eminently curable and in some cases now completely eradicated.

Cholera

*Cholera is an acute infection caused by the **Vibrio Cholerae** bacteria resulting in severe and acute diarrhoea, vomiting, thirst, severe dehydration, kidney failure, sunken eyes and shrivelled skin. Despite the list of complications cholera can be mild or even without symptoms but it can also be severe and life threatening. The bacteria is transmitted through infected water and food, particularly shellfish and Eastbourne was very famous for its oyster trade, and the resulting bacteria contained in diarrhoea can go on to infect particularly water courses. In Victorian England it was often found that human waste overflowed from basement cesspits or open drains into water courses and then into shared water pumps or water pipes.*

At the time the predominant theory was that the illness, the bacteria was not known at the time, was spread though poisonous vapours that contained particles of decaying matter, the so called MIASMA theory. In 1854 John Snow identified one outbreak in London, a city that was particularly badly affected due to the poverty and overcrowding, and isolated the source to a single public water pump that was contaminated by a leaking sewer. The pump was shut down and the number of cases of cholera fell. The contradiction at the time was that when good sanitation was installed the disease disappeared and this was considered to be due to the air being cleansed thus supporting the miasma theory. The fact that the drinking water was actually cleansed and no was no longer contaminated was not considered, by some, to be the reason for the fall in cases.

In 1849 there were 53,293 deaths due to cholera reported, in 1854 there were 20,097 and in 1866 this had fallen to 14,378 cases with the conclusion being that cholera was becoming less destructive. Nevertheless in 1866 it was suggested that, without wishing to alarm anyone, attention was called to the fact that cholera, in a severe form, was spreading in various parts of the country. In one week there had been 346 deaths from cholera in London, a well-known hot spot for the disease. It was considered that there would have to be some time to elapse before the cholera could be cleared from the country and in the meantime wholesome food, pure air and cleanliness were the best preventatives. Again in 1883, and again without indulging in any alarming phrases the link between the water supply and the spread of cholera was raised. It was considered beyond doubt that water contaminated with sewage would induce cholera in any persons who may happen to partake in it. Of course an absolute necessity was to have perfectly pure drinking water and this could be had by drinking Ellis's Ruthin Waters. Visitors to the seaside and elsewhere were advised to avoid the ordinary drinking water and insist on having Ellis's water.

At an Eastbourne Vestry meeting in 1871 Dr Jeffrey hoped that cholera would not break out in Eastbourne but he thought that the people would do all in their power to keep it from the town. Eastbourne was thought to have certain advantages in that regard with Mr Dexter remarking that Eastbourne with its pure, salubrious air and natural advantages would maintain a clean bill of health. This was also remarked on in 1883. With cholera seen to be loosening its grip it would behove every household to see that no predisposing causes of illness should be allowed to remain on their premises any longer than necessary. The fact that Eastbourne had good drainage, pure breezes, wide spaces and broad roads interspersed with a profusion of verdure would help to keep the town healthy.

In 1881 Dr H.D. Ellis observed that there was nowhere with more cheerful surroundings than Eastbourne, nowhere where the sun's rays reflected themselves better than in Eastbourne. But he was somewhat more accurate when he noted that Eastbourne had the best sanitary arrangements that could be found – a sanitary system that was considered to be the most perfect in the kingdom. That was what was probably saving Eastbourne. Certainly Lewes in 1892 hoped that the cholera would not extend to the county but they lived under the happy assurance that they enjoyed a plentiful water supply which was considered to be the greatest preventative against cholera spreading.

Knight, Clark and co. the Westham Nursery in Langney suggested that cholera could be avoided by growing your own fruit instead of buying stale fruit as had been done. They offered strong, healthy pear, apple, cherry and plum trees for

1/6d each. But what else could be done to stop the disease spreading? This question was asked in 1892 with the answer being to see everywhere scrupulously clean and the best way to secure perfect cleanliness was to use Sunlight soap. It was recommended by medical men, officers of health and professional disinfectors and trained nurses.

If the soap did not work and you did contract the disease what could be done? Confinement, bed rest and hydration were the best courses of action but there were plenty of other treatments available. In 1866 Dr J Collis Browne, late of the army medical staff, offered Chlorodyne as an effective cure for cholera, dysentery and diarrhoea but beware if it did not have the words "Dr J Collis Browne's Chlorodyne" as the Government stamp it was not genuine. Come 1894 and the original and only true Freeman's Chlorodyne for colds, cancer, toothache and cholera was on the market and obviously had a very wide range of effectiveness. Its trade mark was the "Elephant" on the wrapper as well as the words "Freeman's Original Chlorodyne" engraved on the Government stamp. Without these it would be an imposter.

In 1873 B.K. Earnshaw the English and Foreign chemist of Victoria Place offered the Anti-Cholera mixture which was recommended but not described by the Board of Trade. It was for immediate use in all cases of diarrhoea, cholera and all disorders of the stomach and bowels. This, indeed was a problem for the Victorian medical men. How to tell the difference between the numerous causes of diarrhoea. Was it food poisoning, dysentery or cholera or just an upset stomach? Fortunately Harmer's Diarrhoea and Cordial mixture from A.D.Harmer and son, chemists of South Street and 3 Buckingham Place, Seaside was an invaluable remedy for cholera, diarrhoea, griping pains, spasms, sickness, dysentery and all bowel complaints. Perhaps you did not trust the proprietary solutions then make your own using 5 grains of brassica every day, in the morning, on the tongue with 5 grains of viscum in the evening. This could be obtained from Dr COUNT MAZETTI in Islington and despite being sufficient to protect against contagious diseases it contained no poisons.

Diphtheria

*Diphtheria is a highly contagious infection caused by the **Corynebacterium Diphtheriae** bacteria that secretes toxins into the body. It presents with a high temperature and a very sore throat which has a thick grey white coating covering the back of the throat, nose and tongue which can significantly constrict breathing hence the disease also being known as the Strangling Angel of Children.*

The Medical Officers of Health regularly published health reports for Eastbourne cataloguing the numbers of births and deaths in the town either by quarter or by the year and Eastbourne was often shown to be the least affected by infectious disease when compared with other coastal or inland towns. Diphtheria was also shown to be one of the least fatal diseases in the town. In 1879 there were 8 deaths recorded with diphtheria compared with 102 from scarlet fever, in 1880 there were 11 diphtheria deaths compared with 120 deaths from whooping cough and in 1882 with a population of around 25,000 and 143 deaths of children under the age of 5 with the youngest being only 10 minutes old there were only 2 deaths from diphtheria.

In 1894 it was suggested that the very low, overall, death rate in Eastbourne would put the Sanitary Committee out of a job and it was suggested they might turn their attention to the banning of kissing. It had been postulated that kissing was unhygienic and that people should desist as much as possible to reduce the spread of infection. The claim was that Princess Alice, daughter of Queen Victoria, had died of diphtheria in 1878 at the age of 38 from kissing one of her 4 children who had caught the disease. This proved the fact that kissing was dangerous and the 'beslobbering' of children could not be too strongly condemned on hygienic grounds. This had been raised in 1888 when a doctor had noted it was possible that diphtheria resulted from kissing although he went on to suggest that was the least ill that kissing could bring about. His view was that the worst disease contracted by a young man who devoted several nights week to labial exercise frequently terminated in a violent case of matrimony. He considered that although this was less dangerous than diphtheria it was considered to be more expensive and likely to hang on much longer.

As with all the infectious diseases prevention was considered to be the order of the day. Izal, a non-poisonous disinfectant, was claimed to be the safest and surest protector against fevers and diphtheria. It was an entirely new discovery that was more easily distributed though water than carbolic acid and four times more powerful with no inconvenience or danger. A 2/6d bottle could make 30 gallons of reliable disinfectant. In 1877 it was advised that a child should never go to sleep with cold feet. Neglect of this would often result in dangerous attacks of croup, fatal sore throats and diphtheria. Mothers were advised that if children were coming home with wet or cold feet the socks and shoes should be removed and the feet warmed by the fire with reserve shoes and stockings kept ready for use at a minutes notice. But if even with warm feet diphtheria was contracted how should it be treated? There were, of course, plenty of options but perhaps not the one reported from Newfoundland in 1898. There, the father who claimed he did not know what to do with his sons who had caught the disease greased the throat inside with a candle and tied a split herring around the throat. Surprisingly and probably not due to the efforts of the herring the eldest son survived only to die later of starvation.

But as with any disorder the pharmaceutical industry was there to help. In 1886 Holloway's ointment was able to cure bronchitis, coughs, colds and diphtheria because it was a sovereign remedy for all derangements of the throat and chest. However Frazer's Sulphur tables, which reassuringly contained no poisons, would cleanse and cool feverish blood by allaying any unhealthy ferment in 1890. Being an antiseptic and germ destroyer it would ward off fevers, measles and diphtheria. Not only that but it was safe and suitable for women and children.

This must have been quite an improvement on the treatment advocated by a Dr Field in 1879 who had used a wonderful cure for diphtheria. He used a teaspoon of flower of brimstone (sulphur) in a wine glass of water stirred by the finger and not a spoon as a gargle for the patient. As brimstone was known to kill off every fungus in man it would clear diphtheria in 10 minutes. To make sure the diphtheria was eradicated the brimstone could be swallowed after gargling instead of spitting it out. But one of the symptoms of diphtheria was that the throat could close down through swelling making it difficult to gargle. In this case sulphur could be blown down the throat using a quill. If even that was not possible then a hot coal should be placed on a shovel and a spoonful or two of flower of brimstone should be sprinkled over it and the vapours inhaled. If that all seemed a little risky then in 1879 Dr Churchill's Hypophosphites and Stoechiological inhalants could cure loss of voice and diphtheria.

In the same year, 1879, treatment became much more scientific. Dr J Abernethy Hicks, an Eastbourne doctor wrote an article in the *Lancet* regarding his treatment of diphtheria. Being the Civil Surgeon in charge of HM Military Hospital in Eastbourne, he advocated the use of Sesquichchloride combined with chlorate of potash and Duncan Flockhart's chloric ether. He claimed iron was pivotal in the treatment and that mercury should be avoided. If emetic treatment was required then ipecacuanha powder with sesquicarbonate of ammonia was to be used. If an aperient was required the hydragogue cathartic known as jalap powder was to be used. If you did not have any of the ingredients to hand in the medicine cabinet, and who would, perhaps the local chemist could oblige. Sadly alcohol as a treatment was to be avoided but it was suggested that a good port wine could have been of great benefit. For the afflicted nutrition in the form of Brand's essence with cream, milk and eggs would suffice washed down with a chlorine drink with lemon and a little syrup was recommended.

Dr Abernathy Hicks treatment sounded very scientific but perhaps more recognisable science was on the way. In 1899 Dr Doting experimented with formaldehyde gas in air tight steel containers. He found that it killed off diphtheria that had been rubbed on blankets and this was even more effective when placed in a steamer. The famous doctor Elizabeth Garrett Anderson and those that studied the disease were a little more puzzled over diphtheria in 1897 although in 1883 Arthur Conan Doyle wrote in his treatise *Life and Death in Blood* that the scientific world was striving to solve the infectious diseases and it was hoped that in the days of the scientist's children's children diseases like diphtheria would have ceased to exist.

Help was on the way and in 1894 the Metropolitan Asylums Board were considering the propriety of adopting the new inoculation for diphtheria in patients in hospitals under their management. However, perhaps not surprisingly after the furore over small pox vaccinations, anti-vaccinationists were against it but also, this time, anti-vivisectionists were also against it claiming that the research had been done on horses.

As with small pox there were anti-vaxers in Eastbourne and one was present on the platform at a meeting in New Hall. They disbelieved in the system of vaccination and were on a mission to enlist others who were anxious to bring about mitigation of the dire evil. They claimed that vaccination did not lessen the malady but had the effect of spreading it and rendering it more mischievous.

Measles

*Measles is a highly contagious viral disease caused by a virus in the **Paramyxovirus** family. It is passed through direct contact and through the air. It affects the respiratory tract and presents with high fever, running nose, white spots inside the cheek with a rash developing over the face and upper neck.*

Measles, perhaps surprisingly was a very serious infectious disease resulting in many deaths. In 1877 there were 121 deaths from measles and in 1880 48 deaths compared with 8 from small pox. In 1884 the unusually high death rate in Eastbourne was put down in great measure to measles and diarrhoea. As a back handed compliment in 1899 it was stated that the fame of the fair town of Eastbourne had spread far and wide and the desire to see Eastbourne was as catching as measles.

Measles was particularly prevalent amongst children. In 1898 the Polegate school was closed in the June because of the spread of measles. In 1899 one man was summonsed for non-payment of a 10 shilling instalment but he claimed that all ten of his children had suffered with measles as had he. But there may have been money to be made. In 1880 one gentleman whose son had had measles suggested that the doctor who treated him should offer a 10% reduction in his bill because all the boy's friends had all contracted the disease and had been attended by the same doctor increasing the doctor's business considerably.

As usual Wright's Coal Tar soap was the preventative to stop the spread of measles but it had competition in 1879 from Dr Barry's Delicious Revalenta Arabica food. This was health without medicine and treated 49 different diseases, everything from noises in the ears to hysteria and measles. It could also overcome all infantile difficulties such as teething and, of course, measles. But users had to be cautious as they were warned that speculators had puffed up all kinds of cheap and worthless foods but the genuine Arabica food was worth its weight in gold.

Just to confuse matters it was found in 1863 that a large proportion of Irish pigs had the larvae of a tapeworm. When a butcher sought to buy pigs he engaged the services of a "measles trier" because every pig had measles and if they did their value was reduced. The measles trier would make incisions in the pig's tongue and rump muscles to look for larvae. It was claimed 50,000 pigs in Ireland had the larvae and they could be particularly transmitted to people who ate raw pork because it "improved the wind".

Scarlet Fever

*Scarlet fever or as it is sometimes called Scarletina is caused by a **Group A Streptococcus** which releases a toxin. The disease features a bright red rash that covers most of the body together with a high fever and sore throat with difficulty in swallowing and enlarged glands in the neck. It is most common in children between the ages of 5 and 15 and can last, without treatment for 2 to 3 weeks.*

In 1872 Eastbourne was noted for maintaining a high state of salubrity which placed her at the head of English watering places as regards health. With a population of 12,954 and 10,000 visitors it reported only 45 deaths for the quarter preceding November. Of these 12 were infants below the age of 1 and 12 were aged over 60. None of the deaths were from small pox, measles, diphtheria or scarlet fever. This was despite it being claimed in 1870 that scarlet fever had overtaken small pox as being excessively fatal although it was noted it was difficult to hedge it in. By 1884 Eastbourne was boasting almost total immunity from scarlet fever with only two deaths in the previous 18 months. It was said this statistic spoke highly of the efficiency in which the sanitary arrangements of the town were carried out.

Whether there were many deaths or not the mere suggestion of the presence of scarlet fever could cause a problem for the town. In 1882 it was claimed that some 16 or 17 years previously scarlet fever had broken out around Cavendish Place and Victoria Place. This had been reported in the *Telegraph* and

Times newspapers and it gave world-wide publicity to something Eastbourne would have preferred to keep quiet. As there had been several deaths a panic ensued and all who could escape Cavendish Place did so with as many as 200 families leaving in a single day. The outbreak was contained although a family in Old Town was affected by taking in infected washing. But the problem was that the fever was being talked about and the town was reported to have suffered a bad name for several years.

Precautions against the spread of a highly contagious disease were the order of the day. In 1889 Dr Fussell, the Chief Medical Officer of Health in Eastbourne insisted when visiting cottages with scarlet fever that the patient had a sheet placed over his head and face and the windows of the room opened for five minutes before he would enter the room. If he did not have a glazed mackintosh with him he used a sheet instead and apologised to friends and family for keeping his hat on. Presumably a Victorian form of the personal protective equipment that has become familiar. In 1893 a father visiting from Notting Hill was summoned by the Sanitary Committee for taking his child who was suffering from scarlet fever from the house they were staying in in Beltring Road through the streets in a cab and on the train to London exposing the public to danger of infection. He was fined 40s. But it did work the other way around. In 1885 a gentleman in Guy's Hospital advertised for apartments in Eastbourne for himself and his wife with a sitting room and large bedroom so he could convalesce from scarlet fever.

In 1881 there was an exhaustive description of the precautions that should be taken when dealing with a case of scarlet fever and a detailed account of the treatment that should be given. It was recognised as being a highly contagious disease and that everything that was thrown off from the body of an infected person was heavily laden with germs or seeds capable of propagating the disease. The discharges from the nose, mouth and bowels were considered to be particularly virulent. If those discharges were to find their way into the cesspools or sewers they could give off poison to the surrounding air.

The instructions for treatment were:

1) Clear the room of all needless woollen or other draperies such as carpets, curtains, wardrobes and chests of drawers as they might harbour the poison. (The cause of the disease had not yet been discovered). The doorway could have a curtain constantly moistened with carbolic acid hung over it.

2) A basin of chlorinated lime or convenient disinfectant should be kept for the patient to spit into.

3) A large vessel with water impregnated with chlorides or Condy's fluid should be available for all bed and body linen taken from the patient. (Condy's fluid was an aqueous solution of calcium and potassium permanganate).

4) Small pieces of rag and not handkerchiefs should be used to wipe the nose and it could be cleaned with a camel hair brush or a syringe with Condy's fluid.

5) Two basins, one with Condy's fluid and one with plain soap and water should be available for hand washing.
6) All glasses, cups and other utensils used by the patient should be scrupulously cleaned.
7) Discharges from the bowels or kidneys should be received as they were issued into vessels charged with disinfectants.

After the fourth day the skin should be oiled with olive oil and a little carbolic acid until the patient could take a warm bath with disinfectant soap and warm water which should be taken every other day for four days. The patient should not think of stirring from their room for three weeks and could not be considered to be free from the disease until his skin had stopped peeling. Once cured the patient could be dressed in a complete set of clean clothes and might then mingle with friends without being considered an object of terror by them.

If all that was too much trouble then in 1879 Brandreth's pills which were conceded by medical men as being the best cleansing medicine with only one pill being needed to clean 30 feet of intestine and preventing reabsorption which was a fearful cause of suffering. It was also beyond value in scarlet fever as well as sea sickness and rheumatism. If you did not need purging then Wright's Coal Tar soap, which was prescribed by the entire medical profession and available everywhere, would protect from small pox, measles and scarlet fever.

Small Pox

*Small pox is an acute contagious disease caused by the **Variola** virus. It could be a deadly disease killing millions and causing permanent scarring and disfigurement for survivors before it was eradicated. The symptoms were fever, nausea, muscle and headaches with fatigue in the incubation period moving to the formation of flat red spots forming at first in the throat and mouth and then over the body. These blisters fill with fluid and then pus before forming scabs which eventually fall off leaving pitted scarring. It is spread by coughs and sneezes and contact with skin sores and was fatal in 30% of cases.*

Throughout history and around the world small pox appeared periodically and this was the case in England although Eastbourne was very fortunate in not experiencing large numbers of cases. Nevertheless Eastbourne being Eastbourne and being in line with the rest of the country the issue of vaccination against small pox was a subject that attracted a great deal of attention and argument.

In 1871 it was remarked that Eastbourne had been marvellously free from the fearful ravages of small pox. In did say that there no cases in 1872 despite a population of around 15,703 one death in 1874, one in 1887. Despite the low number of cases it was decided to build a small pox hospital specifically for the isolation of small pox cases however it was little used throughout its history. The freedom from disease was contrasted with the high incidence of the disease in London and other large towns from which Eastbourne and other watering places drew their visitors. This immunity was laid at the table of Providence and the natural advantages of Eastbourne such as the invigorating and bracing air, pure and plentiful water, wide and open streets and effective drainage. Nevertheless lodging house keepers were cautioned in the reception of their invalid visitors. They were reminded that no lodging that had been exposed to infection was allowed to reopen without a disinfection certificate.

Because of the low number of cases in 1893 it was suggested that the inhabitants of Eastbourne had little personal experience of small pox. They were reminded that in its unmodified form small pox was, perhaps, the most terrible of infectious diseases – virulent, contagious, fatal in an enormous number of cases, loathsome in nature and leaving permanent disfigurement and defects in survivors. It was claimed half those affected would die and it was recognised that there was no cure so all efforts had to be directed to prevention.

For prevention then in 1885 nothing was better than Wright's Coal Tar soap which was prescribed for the prevention of small pox by the entire medical profession but, as usual, purchasers should refuse all valueless imitations introduced by unprincipled shopkeepers for extra gain. Whether it was better than the 1877 Albion Milk and Sulphur soap which was a thoroughly pure and disinfecting product and was the best preventative of small pox was not discussed. Outside the bathroom, which most of the houses at the time did not have, iodine placed in a small box with a perforated lid would, in

1867, destroy organic poisons in a room and it could be used to great benefit on cases of small pox. If you felt a more medically orientated treatment was required then the Lamplough Pyretic Saline as recommended by Dr Wilson in 1886 was probably for you. If was claimed to be efficient in disorders such as headache, excitement and small pox and was considered to prevent more disease than any other medicine as well as removing the ill effects of excessive eating and drinking. Once again users were reminded to beware of injurious imitations.

Whether it was the soap, the bracing air or luck Eastbourne was spared much of the trauma experienced by other towns but it did experience a huge amount of debate, argument and conflict over vaccination against small pox and, in particular, the mandatory vaccination of children.

In 1877 there was an anti-vaccinators meeting held at Diplocks Assembly rooms in Terminus Road about the compulsory vaccination of children where it was claimed that 75% of Eastbourne was hostile to vaccinations. This was contrary to the claim in 1880 that anti-vaccinators in Eastbourne were a comparatively small body which claimed to know much more about the matter than the great multitude who believed in the system. A vociferous and potentially ill-informed minority. In 1884 it was claimed they were a miserably small number with insignificant influence.

Ill-informed or not they brought forward many arguments against vaccinations. The cost of mass vaccination was seen to be a problem. The Countess of Noailles, Helena, who lived in

Meads pointed out in 1883 there were children in Ireland living on seaweed when money was being spent on vaccines. In 1867 anti-vaccinators had claimed that upwards of 20,000 had died of small pox in England and Wales between 1863 and 1865 but where one person died at least ten had caught it and recovered. If the cost of vaccination was 5d per person money would be lost following the incompetent manner in which the Vaccination Act was carried out. It was suggested the medical fraternity and clergy were keen for vaccinations because they were being paid to administer it. In 1883 a report from London said that the public vaccinators gave better protection than the vaccinations provided by private practitioners and it suggested the death rate from privately vaccinated upper class children and their running a greater risk of contracting small pox was striking. Credit should be given to the public vaccinators. Even Edward Jenner who had discovered the process was accused by the anti-vaccinators of receiving £30,000 from the Government for his obnoxious system of vaccination and in a crowded meeting in 1884 in Wadey's Assembly rooms it was claimed that the system was costing £14,800 a year to administer. It was suggested that the inhabitants of Eastbourne would do well at the next Guardians elections to elect more members who would guard and protect the poor instead of spending money on poisoning children

Aside from the cost the meeting was told that the epidemics in London were down to the insanitary arrangements in the city and the fact was that small pox was rarely known in the rural areas of Sussex. The chairman of the meeting denounced

182

vaccination as an obnoxious system and he questioned why there had not been an uprising of the multitude against the diabolical custom. In 1893 it was claimed that pre-vaccination the mortality in London from small pox was forty times greater than they were post vaccination but this was due to better sanitation not vaccination. But it was pointed out that the incidence in children who had been vaccinated had fallen but the cases of other infectious diseases had not fallen in children despite improvements in sanitation. The reduction in infant mortality had to be due to vaccination.

But as in all of these discussion statistics of dubious authenticity were continually brought forward. In 1895 it was claimed that doubly vaccinated soldiers died at twice the rate of unvaccinated men and it was time to give up the quackery and humbug of vaccinations. In was also said that Jenner had claimed it was impossible to have small pox if a person was vaccinated. It was said this was untrue and the speaker defied all the doctors in the universe to prove that vaccination even prevented small pox or assisted to relieve any person suffering from it. The pro-vaccine lobby was slightly handicapped when it was discovered that the vaccine only gave protection for twelve months and a second vaccine was required. This was taken to prove that the vaccine did not work and a speaker at a meeting in Eastbourne in 1877 counselled that the residents should avoid an alliance with the powers of filth (vaccines) and trust only in the cleanliness of air, of home, of living and of the blood.

At the very least in 1878 the Vaccination Act was seen to be a thief robbing a man of his right to private judgement of his liberty and property. Doctors and the clergy were said to be seen to be hand in glove waving the Bogey of small pox over the heads of the population when small pox was no worse than other fevers if skilfully treated but silly women got frightened and clung to the medical and clerical guides like lunatics.

There were two other sides to small pox. In 1883 it was said that Irish conspirators were sending linen infected with small pox to ladies whose husbands had made themselves obnoxious to the National party. Germ warfare.

On the other hand a doctor reported that a man had sent him a letter saying he had small pox and wanting a consultation. On seeing him the doctor diagnosed rheumatism and not small pox and asked why the man had put small pox in his letter. The reply was "there wasn't a soul in the house that knew how to spell rheumatism."

Typhoid

Typhoid or as it was commonly called the "Filth Disease" is a highly contagious disease caused by the bacteria **Salmonella Typhi** *which was commonly found in contaminated food and water. It presented more slowly than cholera but the patient exhibited a high fever, weakness, stomach pains, diarrhoea or constipation with the potential for a rose coloured rash on the body. Without any treatment it would get worse with the risk of threatening complications and, potentially, death. Indeed* *typhoid killed Prince Albert, Queen Victoria's husband in 1861. In a similar way to cholera it would spread in infected water which could also be infected from poor sanitation, a lack of cleanliness and the presence of the bacteria in the patient's excreta.*

As with Cholera the exact method of transmission of the disease was poorly understood with confusion between the miasma theory and the potential for inadequate sanitation. In 1874 it was considered unlikely that typhoid could be contracted from a chance whiff of sewer gas in the open air but it was stated that there was evidence that sewer gas could find its way into good and well built houses with the probability that typhoid could make its reappearance. There was disappointment that the Eastbourne Local Board publication giving householders sanitary hints to prevent contagious diseases seemed largely to be ignored. Although Eastbourne was eventually to have an efficient and well regarded sewerage and water system it was not always so. In 1877 the drainage of Meads, in particular, was of great concern. There were letters complaining that the drains from the All Saints Convalescent Hospital discharged into a field. If that was not bad enough there were complaints that a farm yard, possibly opposite the Ship Hotel in Meads, had been converted into a cesspool. The smell from the installation found its way as far as the coastguard station. It was suggested that the price to pay for such a system of waste disposal was the appearance of typhoid. Aside from the health risk to the residents it was suggested that people who were seeking a watering place or a seaside resort in search of health were very sensitive and intensely alarmed at the barest whisper of bad drainage. It was claimed, in rather flowery and graphic terms, that potential visitors to Eastbourne would shun the suspected spot as if it were a charnel house or an open grave waiting for them.

The difficulty was knowing what to do with human sewage if there was no effective disposal system. In 1891 it was suggested that it a cesspool could not be abolished or if there was no garden the ash or earth closet should be made shallow enough so that it could be frequently emptied and only so closed to prevent it being constantly filled with rain water. Gradually the drainage systems in Eastbourne improved and so did the clean water supply. In 1896 the new supply of drinking water from Holywell was reported as being greatly appreciated by resident and visitors. As a result the water company was urged to distribute the Holywell water to the central and east wards by means of water vans which could be stationed at various points at fixed hours. If you were too busy to collect your Holywell water then you could try KRYSTAL table water or WESTONER natural seltzer which was the very best and purest in the water. Sold in all leading hotels and chemists it would remove the fear of contracting typhoid. If you were prepared to take your chances with the Holywell water you could perhaps use a Pasteur filter which removed impurities and caused the fear of typhoid to disappear. Simmons and Winfield in 102 Terminus Road in 1898 were the sole agents for the Pasteur and Chamberlain filters which would prevent all fevers and water borne diseases. Hopefully they were an improvement on the filters of 1884 when it was suggested that the protection through filtration was a fallacy unless they were frequently and thoroughly cleaned. If this was not done the filters would become a storehouse and even a factory for poisonous germs and noxious matter capable of producing typhoid fever.

In a familiar war of words anti-vaccinationists, who were vehemently against the small pox vaccination programme, claimed that the improvements in sanitation, that were particularly prevalent in Eastbourne, were the cause of the fall in the number of small pox victims and not the Jenner cow pox vaccine. But there were claims that the improvements in sanitation had not reduced the incidence of typhoid. Indeed some authorities believed that the system of mains drainage was more pernicious to health than the old elementary cesspool.

Whatever the cause the spread of the disease had to be recorded and in 1889 under the Infectious Diseases Notification Act of 1889 notice was given that the head of the family or nearest relation to a typhoid patient should, as soon as they became aware of the situation whether it be typhoid, small pox, cholera, diphtheria, erysipelas (otherwise known as St Anthony's Fire, a disease caused by *Streptococcus pyogenes* resulting in bright red, swollen patches of skin with fever and chills with the potential for gangrene) or scarlet fever should inform the Medical officer of Health. The penalty for not doing so was a 40s fine.

Eastbourne was fortunate, for whatever reason, to avoid the worst of the infectious diseases prevalent at the time. In 1894 there was only one death from infectious disease compared with up to 50 in other south east towns and there were no deaths from typhoid. This was an improvement on 1884 when there were four deaths out of the population of 27,000. Two were attributed to sanitary defects in the home, one was a three year old and another arrived in the town "somewhat indisposed". In case there was any other indisposition in 1884 the people of Eastbourne were encouraged to act with courage and not quake with fear – to prepare for danger with confidence that precautions would reduce the extent of any disease. Perhaps one of the precautions was to stop eating the Eastbourne speciality, oysters, as a medical journal was accused of alarming people claiming there was proof of a connection between eating oysters and typhoid. The claim, unsurprisingly, had a marked effect on consumption.

Whooping Cough

*Whooping cough, also known as pertussis, is a highly contagious disease infecting the lungs and air ways caused by the **Bordetella pertussis** bacteria usually affecting children with babies and young infants being the worst affected. The symptoms which can last for three months or more are repeated coughing bouts, in between which the patient may struggle for breath and make the characteristic whooping sound, runny nose, red eyes, sore throat and slight fever. Patients would be* *isolated because the disease was spread on the droplets of the cough and sneezes.*

Whooping cough was, perhaps, not seen as such a deadly disease as small pox or typhoid but it was actually more deadly. In 1878 there were 13 deaths from whooping cough in what was called a severe epidemic. In 1886 there were eight deaths but only 3 from measles. In 1889 there were 18 deaths from whooping cough but only 4 from typhoid.

As with all the infectious diseases there was no knowledge of the causes of the disease nor any cure. Neither was there any effective treatment other than isolation of the patient and time. Not that the lack of effective treatments stopped any number of 'treatments' being marketed.

During this period there were many advertisements for 'cures' for all and various disorders that could be obtained by sending stamps to various addresses around the country and in return an explanation of the disease and/or a cure or treatment would be sent on trust. Quite how many were scams with nothing being returned to the sender or completely useless products or treatments being sent out of all proportion to the value of the stamps being sent is not recorded but there must have been a degree of fraud. For example in 1883 "The Positive Cure" for whooping cough was available on sending stamps to AJ Heald in Burnham, Buckinghamshire.

If you were somewhat circumspect about mail order solutions physical treatments were to hand. In 1889 no household should be without Children's Cough Syrup. Despite being always useful it was also perfectly harmless which must have been comforting. It was specially prepared for children by B K Earnshaw the English and Foreign chemist in the Victoria Pharmacy, Victoria Place. If you wanted something that was extensively used by medical men at home and abroad then you would use Freeman's Chlorodyne. Never forget Wright's Coal Tar soap either. But medicines of whatever formulation might seem somewhat historic compared with the 1877 Halls' Medicated Voltaic Electric Perforated plasters. They were described as being a perfect self-charged, self-acting electro galvanic battery. In combination with the world renowned medicated perforated plasters they formed a curative agent unsurpassed by any medical discovery of the century. The benefit was said to be miraculous in many conditions including fractured ribs, nervous pains of the bowels stitch in the back and whooping cough.

Eastbourne Health - Nurses and Midwives

Nurses

The definition of the term "nurse" in Victorian England was very broad encompassing a multitude of competency levels. There was the beginning of what we might recognise as a highly trained and qualified person delivering health care in an institution such as a hospital or nursing home. But there also private nurses engaged to look after a single patient in their home, a nurse engaged to look after a community much like a modern day district nurse possibly sponsored by a church or charity, a blend of a role looking after the health and comfort or a person within a family but also helping the woman of the house with household chores to a person better described as a nanny or person delivering child care but not health care. OF course, in the early stages the nurse in the work house might just have been another inmate with no training or expertise at all. Whatever role the woman, and it was almost always a woman, played under the title of "nurse" there was an enormous demand for their services. The papers were filled with huge numbers of advertisements for nurses with myriad job descriptions and nurses advertising their particular services. In addition to the private adverts there were also a number of employment agencies that specialised in the "service" industries such as nursing or scullery maids.

If you needed a German speaking nurse in 1884 then the Eastbourne Servants Agency could supply a 24 year old nurse who could 'talk' English for £18 to £20 and as a bonus she was fond of children and a good needle woman. The Capeltons International agency in 11 Colonnade was a Bureau de Placement for English and Foreign nurses in 1881. In 1888 the Medical and Surgical Home and Institute for Private nurses was conducted by Miss Butterworth from 25 Jevington Gardens promising to supply thoroughly trained nurses at the shortest notice for all cases. The Eastbourne and Sussex Registry Office in 4a Pevensey Road was one such agency offering to place cooks, housemaids, footmen, ladies maids, scullery maids and nurses who wanted situations in 1889. In the same year the Royal Victoria Institute in 104 Terminus Road, which claimed to be the oldest servants agency in Eastbourne could offer nurses for London, the country and abroad. To keep it in the family, in 1885, the daughter of a medical man opened an Institution for Private nurses in Eastbourne and was happy to supply members of the medical profession with efficient and well trained nurses. She was to be the Lady Superintendent and operated out of 44 Grove Road. It was interesting to note that over time the status of the nurse very gradually increased from being comparable to a scullery maid to being a more professional, trained health care provider.

Despite the plethora of agencies seeking to place nurses there were still many, many adverts for and by nurses looking for situations and these ranged over a wide range of definitions of the title - nurse.

They ranged from an advert in 1866 advertising the services of a young 20 year old woman with plenty of milk and a good medical certificate as a wet nurse. Moving up the age range a respectable young country girl was required as a nurse girl in 1896 by Lady Charley in Eastbourne. In 1895 a kind and steady nurse was wanted for young children with good wages at Villa Sphinx in Selwyn Road. A respectable person was wanted at 6 Terminus Road to act as a child nurse and mother's help, a good servant was also kept, with the youngest child being 3 years old. A superior girl aged about 16 was required as a nurse for three children. She was required to be clean, good tempered and have filled a similar position before. As another example of children being employed to look after other children an advert in 1877 wanted a nurse girl of 12 to 14 years who was accustomed to children. Another, also in 1877, wanted a clean, respectable nurse girl of 14-15 years to take care of two or three (the mother seemed a little uncertain) little children and to make herself useful. Nursing care was also required for adults. In 1894 a certified ladies nurse was seeking immediate engagement from 11 Cross Street. In 1895 a highly recommended but disengaged certified nurse with medical and surgical experience wanted a permanent case. Some of the adverts seemed more personal than others. In 1873 a respectable widow with the highest references and otherwise from 22 Bourne Street wished to meet with an invalid desiring comfortable home with careful nursing.

There were bigger employers of nurses in the town and the Eastbourne union was one of them although in 1877 there was great concern about the turn-over of nurses at the workhouse. The point made was that if it carried on Eastbourne would get a bad name so the reasons for the turn-over had to be found.

In 1877 the Guardians of the union met to elect a single woman to fill the office of nurse to the sick and poor in the Union Workhouse and to generally observe the orders and directions of the Local Board. The salary would be £25 with rations. As a result an Ellen Groves from Barnsley was offered the post but she declined having accepted another position. Instead Sarah Murrell was offered the post despite something being heard about her not working harmoniously with the officers in her last position at Wisbeach Union. At the time of the appointment there were 124 inmates with 26 vagrants being admitted. In 1883 a nurse was again required at the Union Infirmary. The candidates were required to be single women or widows without encumbrances between the ages of 25 and 45. They had to be well acquainted with the duties of a midwife with such qualifications being indispensable. The salary was £30 a year with board, lodging and washing included. Applications in the candidates own handwriting with testimonials were required. Help was advertised for in 1890 with the union requiring an assistant nurse for the infirmary. This candidate had to be aged 21 and 35, single or a widow with training or experience in a nursing institution. The salary was £20 a year with apartments in the infirmary and an allowance of 10/6d a week in lieu of rations. In 1886 a nurse was required for the Infectious and Contagious diseases ward at the Union Workhouse and they had to be well acquainted with the duties.

If a nurse wanted to specialise in the infectious diseases area they could, if married to a man who was looking for work as a caretaker, take up a post advertised in 1888 at the Borough Infections hospital. They would be the head (and only) nurse and would be greatly under-worked with very few patients actually passing through the hospital in its history. Just to provide 24 hour care at the workhouse a night nurse was advertised for in 1894. The candidates had to be under the age of 30 again with some training or experience in a nursing institution. In 1891 Miss Wilhelmina Brodie Hall who was a lady member of the Guardians was recognised as having carried out much successful work with orphans of Eastbourne and had also secured the erection of a new infirmary and casual wards as well as securing trained nurses from the Workhouse Infirmary Nursing institute. She was a very successful manager of services but was recognised in 1887 as having secured treacle for the inmates' rice pudding.

If a nurse did not want to work in an institution there were vacancies as a community nurse mainly engaged through church charities. In 1890 a sale of work was advertised at the Christ Church Mission Hall, Lower Drove, Seaside to raise funds for the maintenance of a parish nurse for the east end of town, the least opulent region of Eastbourne. The nurse was seen to be an unspeakable blessing to scores of indigent families. Prior to a similar sale in 1888 the organisers invited friends from the west end to attend and make purchases. The position was found in other districts with All Saints holding an annual Hodge

Podge sale to raise funds to provide a parish nurse to work among the sick in a population of over 5000.

Wherever nurses actually worked the commercial world noted their presence and ability to influence sales. The attention of mothers, nurses and invalids was drawn to Dr Ridge's patent foods for invalids and infants. In 1864 this cooked FARINACEOUS food was claimed to be more nourishing and digestible than any other and was ready for use without trouble in two minutes. It had agents in Victoria Place, Cornfield Road, South Street, Alma Place and Terminus Road. In 1881 Fardon's Nurse Brown's mixture was sold as a real blessing to the infant world. In all cases of teething, wind, colic and sleeplessness the mixture was superior to all others. Colic, wind and gripes could also be cured with Nurse Edda's baby soother. It was an unequalled remedy and, thankfully, entirely free from opiates or noxious or strong medicines. It was therefore guaranteed harmless. It provided instant relief and no-one in charge of a baby should be without it. If the nurse was looking after young children then in 1864 English's Inimitable Teething powders had a marvellous effect and was of great worth as it not only soothed but stopped pain at once. Available from G Mussell, chemist, Pevensey Road.

An alternative to engaging a nurse was to provide one's own nursing cover. In 1885 the St John Ambulance held a course of lectures on nursing at St Saviours Church Rooms in South Street. They were delivered by Mr A P Sherwood and a certificate was publicly distributed to successful candidates. Or in 1888 a course of lectures entitled "Home Nursing" was delivered in the waiting room of the Town hall by Miss Helen Thomson from the hospital for sick children in Birkenhead and a general hospital in Manchester. The shilling and six pence fee for the course did not mention the issuing of a certificate.

It was apparent that advertisements for nurses were beginning to require experience but preferably training and experience in health care institutions. A review of care in workhouses in 1866 demonstrated that the 'Sarah Gamp' was a sad reality. Sarah Gamp was a character in the novel *Martin Chuzzlewit* written by Charles Dickens. It was said she was based on a real character but she was described as an untrained, incompetent dissolute nurse who was sloppy and drunk. The practice of staffing work house infirmaries had been to use pauper inmates who showed an interest in or aptitude for 'nursing' care to provide that level of care to fellow inmates. This served to provide a service but at very little cost not to mention very little benefit. But it was noted that several hospitals had adopted a system of training properly qualified women as nurses. In 1867 the Liverpool Guardians decided that pauper nursing should be abolished in the workhouse infirmary and that staff should be trained in the Nightingale system which would result in more humane treatment. A General Nursing institute had also started with a view to supplying "skilled medical, surgical, fever, mental, monthly* and wet nurses".

There was some condescending backing from doctors who, in 1876, advocated that the medical bias of intelligent women should be diverted to the profession of nursing. They stated that no matter how intensely a woman might pursue surgical knowledge there was not a doubt that in thousands of cases convalescence was due more to the nurses rather than the doctors and that there was more work for nurses than any other profession in the universe. In other words leave the doctoring to the men. They claimed that the need was great in every rank of life and nurses may be efficient whether born as gentle women or peasants.

The Royal British Nurses Association, from the time of its foundation regulated the procedure of an ever increasing number of nurse training schools and it was also authoritatively sanctioned by the House of Lords in Hospital Management as well as establishing a register of trained nurses.

In 1876 Miss Florence Lees, Superintendent General of the Metropolitan and National Association for providing trained nurses to the sick poor and was awarded the Iron Cross by the Emperor of Germany for services to nursing in Germany. She said nursing was becoming more and more recognised as that which it ought always to have been – a profession for educated women. The hospital training now being provided meant that nurses acquired the skills of careful discipline, order, quickness, punctuality, truthfulness, trustworthiness, method, cleanliness neatness and implicit and intelligent obedience to those in authority.

After all that work there was testimony in the magazine the *Christian* to the immense boon that the Eastbourne House of

Rest in Burlington Place on the corner of Compton Street proved to hundreds of tired workers such as toiling hospital nurses and matrons of reformatories and orphanages.

*Monthly nurses: employed short term, usually around a month, to cover a mother's post-natal or post-partum period.

Midwives

Midwifery was not recognised legally until 1902 with an aim of making the profession more accountable and safer for mothers to be. Up until that time women about to give birth had been attended, if they were 'lucky', by local women claiming experience in the mechanics of childbirth. They were perhaps women who had themselves given birth or perhaps women with an interest in the care of pregnant women or maybe just family members.

In the later Victorian period there was a degree of "professionalism" being developed in midwifery. In 1893 there was an advertisement for accouchement (child delivery) services offering a happy home for ladies before and after confinement with a doctor if preferred. Apartments or single rooms were available with every comfort, a piano (presumably viewed as a great benefit in late stages of pregnancy), great cleanliness and good cooking with moderate terms even to invalids. In 1895 there was an advert requesting space in the home of a certified nurse or midwife. But these options were for the wealthy the common, poor folk were much less well catered for and, as a result, midwives often appeared in courts and post mortems explaining the deaths of women in labour and new born babies. In 1864 a woman who admitted she was no sworn midwife but did go out for poor persons as a guinea was a good deal of money for a midwife and she did it for charity. Nevertheless she was called to a woman who was fainting. Despite giving her water and brandy she deteriorated and subsequently died. The post mortem decided she had died of a ruptured uterus and blood loss and it was deemed there was nothing the woman or the doctor could have done to prevent the death.

In 1863 one of the biggest scandals was the finding of baby's bodies in the roof of the Whitechapel Church. Another was the case of a baby declared still-born by the midwife who actually lived for two days after birth. The midwife, who could not write, claimed she had brought 2000 babies into the world. She did not say how many had lived.

Midwifery skills or the lack of them was not the only thing mothers-to-be had to worry about. In 1896 a short, elderly woman described as an unregistered midwife from 9 Fort Road was summoned for unlawfully exposing, without previous disinfection, certain clothing (her wearing apparel) which had been exposed to puerperal fever, a dangerous infectious disorder. The case was dismissed with a caution.

Similarly lightly treated was a Nottingham midwife who was severely reprimanded after ignorantly cutting the tongue of a newly born baby to make it free. The child bled to death.

The authorities were perhaps more selective in the people they employed to deliver midwife service. In 1876 the Guardians of the Eastbourne Union advertised for a duly qualified medical officer and vaccinator for a population of 1480 over 9844 acres with a salary of £95 per annum. They were also to be paid an additional 10/6d for each case of midwifery attended in Alfriston, Litlington and Lullington. For attending cases in Folkington, Jevington and Wilmington they would get an extra 13/0d. In 1882 a medical officer at the Union Workhouse in Eastbourne would get an extra 11/0d for each case and an annual salary of £100.

In 1883 the Guardians wanted a nurse for the Union infirmary. The candidates had to be single or widows without encumbrances between the ages of 25 and 45. They also had to be well acquainted (practically) with the duties of a midwife, such qualities being indispensable. Salary £30 a year with board, lodging and washing.

But the workhouse was not the only place for hospital style care. The Victoria Home run by the Eastbourne Provident Dispensary tabled £43 income from midwifery fees from 100 patients.

Illustrations 14, 15 – Advertisements for nurses

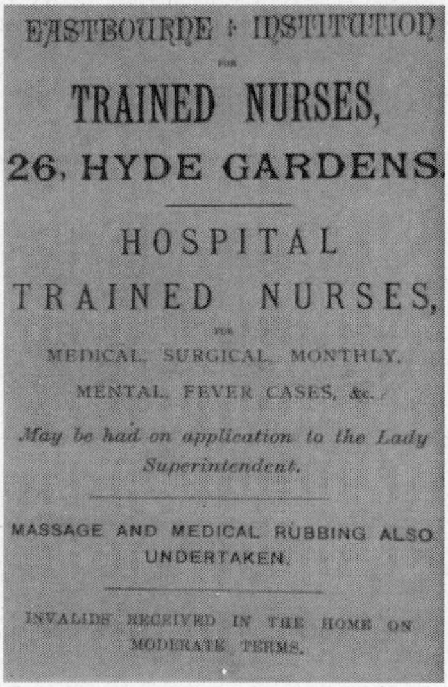

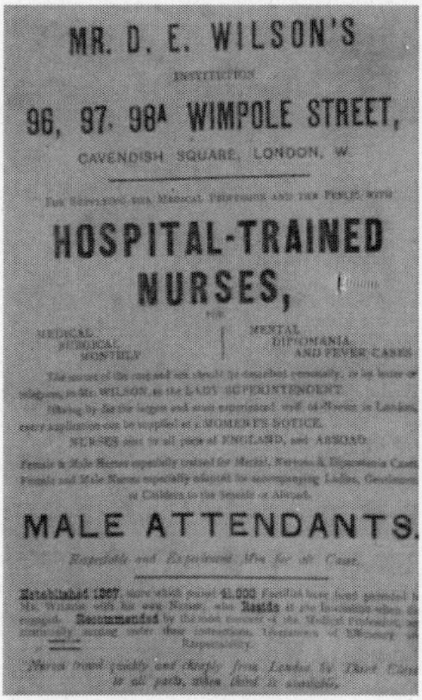

Eastbourne Health - Opticians

A visit to a modern opticians results in extensive testing, highly trained and qualified professionals using a wide range of high tech machinery none of which was available to Victorian optometrists. Indeed optical services were often provided almost as a side line by service providers more interested in selling watches, jewellery, photographic equipment and as with many Victorian entrepreneurs they could diversify as much as R Job of 105A Langney Road who in 1881 advertised as an optician but could also offer umbrella and parasol repair. In 1866 J Miles, albeit of Hastings listed his services as being a cutler, hardware man and, oh yes, an optician.

In 1868 Edward Winder of 4 Terminus Place advertised as a goldsmith, jeweller, watch and clock maker and an optician offering spectacles at 1/- a pair. He was far from alone. W Gilham who claimed to be the oldest established optical firm in Eastbourne operated out of 15 Terminus Road offering a range of optical goods such as opera and field glasses, telescopes, barometers, thermometers and spectacles. F Ciappessoni also a watchmaker, jeweller, silversmith in 3 Victoria Place offered almost as an afterthought opticians services. However in a nod to early diversity he offered repairs in all branches speedily and punctually attended to by English and foreign workers. Some claimed a degree of speciality such as W Sparrow who in 1899 was a manufacturing optician in 16 Pevensey Road claiming spectacles and eye glasses were a speciality. But just in case he also had a large stock of magic lanterns and slides.

Some did specialise. Walter W Whitehouse who in 1898 was also a manufacturing optician in 20 Cornfield Terrace and offered opera, field and marine glasses but also made up spectacles of every description to order on the premises. He demonstrated "highly interesting specimens" of his workmanship at the Optical Exhibition at the Mansion House, London in 1898 which included a pair of spectacles weighing less than 11 grains. As a result he was admitted as a Freeman of the Company of Spectacle makers. By the following year he had DBOA and FSMC after his name and the title ophthalmic optician to the East Sussex Hospital Surgical Aid Society specialising in spectacles and *pince nez*.

Not everyone was quite as expert at least to start with and they also did not necessarily need to actually see a patient. In 1868 a Frederick J Cox of Ludgate Hill offered improved spectacles adapted to defective vision. This was a new system by which residents could be accurately suited without a personal visit and all post free for 13 stamps. But by 1885 a Frederick J Cox was established in 56 Terminus Road offering instruments for electricity, entomology and medical galvanism (the principle used to alleviate insanity by the application of electrical pulses providing muscle contraction), as well as spectacles and eye preservers adapted to old, long or short sight by the Optometer (an early instrument for measuring eyesight) or to the specifications of ophthalmic surgeons. He offered his services with promptitude and accuracy at moderate charges. But by 1896 he was selling off all his photographic equipment as he was going to devote himself entirely to the optical or more especially the spectacle trade.

Spectacles might be considered to be a standard device but not necessarily so in Victorian Eastbourne. The Messer's W Herbert and Godfrey of London with an eye to their desired clientele begged to inform the nobility and gentry of Eastbourne in 1879 that they had appointed Messer's Holttum and Stevens, chemists of 30 Terminus Road as sole agents for their celebrated "Aqua Crystal Spectacles" and "Pebble Spectacles" (Thick round lenses with a high degree of magnification) which were guaranteed to be cut from rock and were strongly recommended by medical men. The Aqua Crystal spectacles were said to possess advantages over other glasses sold. It was claimed they could be used for reading or writing for six hours at a time without straining the eyesight. They did not need repeated cleaning as the natural mist of the eyes did not affect them and sight was relieved by their use instead of causing eyes to ache as glasses frequently did. As if that was not enough they also afforded protection of the eye from heat, light, gas and from variations of the atmosphere. In 1880 Arthur Boots of Susan's Road offered as sole agent "Crystal Periscope" glasses as supplied to Her Most Gracious Majesty Queen Victoria.

Care had to be taken in selecting spectacles. In 1866 E Hayward of 9 Pevensey Road suggested that those who used spectacles were well aware of the value of them but were not always sufficiently careful in the choice of suitable focus having it either too weak or too strong. He had spectacles for long and short sight and he would take care to ensure that the proper focus was delivered. Indeed optics did develop and in 1884 Henry Laurance offered improved spectacles whose manufacture was based on improved but undisclosed principles and were used or recommended by leading oculists and gentlemen of the medical profession. They were clear and cool and never tired the eyes while subduing all inflammatory symptoms while assisting, strengthening and preserving the sight. They were available from Arthur Boots at 65 Cavendish Place and were stamped HL to ensure they were genuine.

Nothing came without a price though however there were alternatives. In 1899 Mr H T Hamblin of 108 South Street offered those whose eyesight was failing or who were troubled by their eyes a consultation with a spectacle specialist. His offer would cost you nothing. Best steel framed glasses suitable for all sights could be purchased from J A Faulkener of 13 Pevensey Road for 1/10d a pair. While there he also claimed to be the cheapest house for wedding and birthday presents. In 1889 William Bruford of 100 Terminus Road, specialists in optics offered real Pebble Spectacles at 2/6d a pair. Of course if you were really poor there was the Eastbourne branch of the Surgical Aid Society who in 1899 distributed, amongst other things, five sets of artificial teeth, 18 trusses and 13 pairs of spectacles.

It was possible to avoid the use of spectacles altogether. In 1876 Dr J Ball and Co. offered Ivory Egg cups which could restore your eyesight and render spectacles useless as all diseases of the eyes could be cured with their use. At advertisement it was claimed over 25,000 persons had been cured using the treatment which could be used without the aid of doctors. The fact that they were small cups with a rubber balloon inside which were placed over the eye with the balloon being inflated to create a vacuum thereby changing the shape of the eyeball might suggest having medical help nearby might be advisable.

If you did not want to get that far then in 1894 if your eyes were weak, sore, inflamed or blood shot you could use a daily bath of Optic Solution which improved weak sight and prevented the need for spectacles for children. Available for 2/9d from Richardson, Specialist, Manchester who would also send valuable information on the eyes.

Illustration 16: Opticians advertisement

PHOTOGRAPHIC, ELECTRIC, AND SCIENTIFIC INSTRUMENTS.

FREDERICK J. COX,

56, TERMINUS ROAD,

Optician and Spectacle Maker.

Spectacles and Eye Preservers adapted to the Requirements of Old, Short, or Weak Sight by the Optometer.

Special attention is given to the careful fitting of the Frames, as well as accuracy in Working to the Specifications of Ophthalmic Surgeons.

PHOTOGRAPHIC APPARATUS, CHEMICALS, DRY PLATES, SENSITIVE PAPERS AND PLATES. Repairs and Alterations of all kinds.

Eastbourne Health - Pharmacies and Dispensaries

Dr Scott's bilious liver pills, Beecham's pills, Frazer's tablets, Kaye's Worsdell's pills, teething powders, Dr Ridge's patent foods, chlorodyne, camomile pills, Powell's balsam. As there appeared to be no end of ailments there was also no end of proprietary medicines all guaranteed to cure a number of completely unrelated but common illnesses most of which had absolutely no benefit whatsoever. The days of understanding the transmission of disease, microbiology, human physiology and detailed anatomy were still ahead. There was little or no pharmacological research and, mainly, absolutely no evidence any of the medicines purveyed to the desperate public worked. Nevertheless there was a great market for such solutions and they could either be acquired through a profusion of mail order advertisements or by popping down to the local pharmacist or dispensary who would offer medical advice instead of consulting a medical man.

The pharmacist would happily supply any of the medicines on the market often being a sole agent for a town but they also provided a service by formulating medicines as prescribed by the doctor. They might prepare medicines such as:

An 1876 mixture for diarrhoea:

Aromatic confection	$1\frac{1}{2}$ drams
Compound tincture of cardamums	4 drams
Aromatic spirit of ammonia	2 drams
Chalk mixture	2 ounces

Distilled water	6 ounces

$\frac{1}{6}$th part to be taken when required (it will not keep for many days)

An 1876 mixture for influenza and cold in the head:

Liquid acetate of ammonia	6 drams
Dilute nitric acid	$1\frac{1}{2}$ drams
Chloric ether	$1\frac{1}{2}$ drams
Distilled water	8 ounces

$\frac{1}{6}$th part to be taken 3 times a day

Throughout history there had been apothecaries who had prepared and sold medicines to fellow citizens suffering from illness and disease but in the Pharmacy Act of 1852 a registry of people trained as pharmacists was set up and, possibly as an oversight, over 200 women pharmacists were registered. In 1868 another Pharmacy Act limited the sale of fifteen poisons and dangerous drugs to qualified pharmacists. Opium, for example, could not be sold in Great Britain unless the container was labelled as a poison and had the name and address of the seller which must have hampered the illegal drug dealers.

So their products might still have been ineffective but at least the pharmacists might have a degree of education, albeit extremely basic, and the pills and potions they sold might have been safer. Perhaps because Eastbourne was seen to be a premier health resort or perhaps because the people of

Eastbourne were supremely entrepreneurial there were soon many pharmacists to choose from and they often advertised their services. Many of the products were based on homeopathic principles and Eastbourne had an active and famous homeopathic hospital, the Leaf Hospital, and a Homeopathic Convalescent home and in 1871 there was the Eastbourne Homeopathic dispensary run by Messers Harmer and son in 6 Richmond Terrace, Susan's Road. It enlisted subscribers of half a guinea or one guinea per annum for which they received four or eight tickets for distribution. The Working Classes who were not able to obtain a subscription card were able to attend the dispensary and obtain medical advice on payment of half a crown a month or one shilling each time they attended. Residents and visitors were respectfully reminded that being the only homeopathic chemist in Eastbourne that genuine homeopathic medicines could only be obtained from Harmers.

In 1881 Geo. J Attenburrow in 2 Compton Street, a family and dispensing chemist offered to faithfully compound physicians prescription or any family recipes that customers swore by. In 1894 George A Harmer in South Street a dispensing and family pharmacist that had been established in 1830 personally conducted dispensing at the lowest reasonable prices with the very lowest prices charged for cash. The Central Pharmacy run by J Gibbs and son in Terminus Road, nearly opposite the Post Office, was a pharmaceutical and homeopathic chemist who also carefully and accurately dispensed drugs, homeopathic or otherwise, of the best quality at reasonable prices from prescriptions supplied by physicians. In 1884 W J Gilbert MPS (Pharmaceutical Chemist by Examination) ensured that medicines would be supplied at such moderate charges as were consistent with absolute purity and that necessary skill (imparted through examination) required in the preparation.

As with all commercial enterprises in Eastbourne it was always good to have a particular edge over the competition. C H Temple of the Regent Pharmacy in 83 South Street not only stocked Temple's anodyne corm plasters which gave instant relief and were prepared and sold only by Temple's but they were also the sole agents for Routly's Indian liver pills. As if that was not enough if you were in the shop on a Wednesday or Saturday you could consult Mr Edgar Power a visiting surgeon dentist from Brighton. Indeed, in the early days, a pharmacists shop was frequently used by visiting part time dental surgeons. Corn competition was to be had from W R Baker Seaside Pharmacy at 91 Seaside. He asked "why suffer any longer from the terrible torment of corns when relief and cure are to be obtained using Baker's marvellous corn cure?"

If you could boast royal patronage then it must be a bonus. B K Earnshaw the English and Foreign chemist in Victoria Pharmacy, Victoria Place announced they were under the patronage of the Royal families of England and Germany namely HRH the Grand Duke of Besse Darmstadt, HRH the Grand Duke of Baden-Baden. If that was not advantage enough the shop also had rooms above that they rented out and one of the more successful renters was the Scientific Dress Cutting Association who ran classes from 10 to 4 and advertised prolifically.

Not all pharmacists restricted themselves to medicines. John Dutton, dispensing and family pharmacist of 51 Terminus Road offered in 1865 French polish reviver, rose tooth powder, marrow pomade and a large assortment of sponges, sponge bags, bathing caps and every toilet requisite as well as being sole agent for German Fir Wool medicines. In 1892 Willan and Co in the Eastbourne Pharmacy adjoining the Town Hall in 69 Grove Road offered Lundberg's famous perfumes such as Goya Lily, Swiss Lilac and Alpine Violet.

But not everything was as sweet smelling in the land of the pharmacy. In 1868 J A Provost opened the Operative and Dispensing pharmacy business in 14 Terminus Road and in his advert he respectfully solicited a share of the favours and patronage of the medical profession and the residents and visitors of Eastbourne. In 1881 Mr Provost stated that the exigencies of an increasing business coupled with inordinate mental strain induced him to seek assistance. In that year Herbert Crook a pharmaceutical chemist and silver medallist of the South London School of Pharmacy joined Mr Provost now at 94 Terminus Road and assured everyone he would give his best attention to the execution of all business confided to the firm. Twelve months later Mr Crook announced he was taking over as active superintendent of the business as Mr Provost was retiring due to the heavy responsibility of a chemist's business and domestic illness and trouble.

There was quite a number of independent pharmacists in the town but it was recognised that there was a large number of impoverished residents whose ability to access medical advice and medicine was severely limited by their poverty. To address this the Homeopathic Dispensary was started at the Workmen's Hall with the honorary secretary being Miss Leaf and the Treasurer Miss J Leaf both heavily involved in the Leaf Homeopathic hospital. Subscribers of one guinea were entitled to six tickets each available for four consultations. Patients could be admitted by the payment of one shilling each time or by a subscription ticket and that would include any medicines prescribed. It was stressed that no patient would be admitted if they were in a position to pay ordinary fees.

Perhaps the more famous dispensary was the Eastbourne Provident Dispensary originally in 36 and 38 Pevensey Road but latterly in Shaftesbury House South Street. This was formed in 1865 after two medical men had failed to start such an institution before. The object of the institution was to enable the working classes to ensure for themselves and their families advice from duly qualified and registered physicians and surgeons and medicine during illness by their own small periodic payments with the assistance of others. It was to be open between 9 and 12 in the morning and 6 and 8 in the evening with urgent cases being attended at any hour of the day or night.

As with many institutions in Eastbourne it was often short of funds and in 1877 the valuable institution was languishing and it was a surprise that the public did not afford it more support. It was recognised it could not be self-supporting and claimed it was the duty of the rich and well-to-do to think of the hard struggle for existence that fell to the lot of their poorer brethren. But it was suggested the management had not taken the necessary steps to promote the dispensary and had carried out their work quietly and unobtrusively. It was essential that the people of Eastbourne came forward with subscriptions particularly as the committee wanted to build a cottage hospital in connection with the dispensary.

Initially a house in Terminus Place was used but the rent proved too much of a strain on the resources and they had to be bailed out by a Mrs Curling. In 1883 Lady Victoria Long Wellesley donated £2000 for the purchase of Benhall House, 49 Cavendish Place, opposite the Congregational Church in Pevensey Road to become the hospital. The house had ample accommodation and also had excellent sanitary arrangements. Alterations were started in 1883 and finished with the hospital opening in 1885. Members attending for medicine had a separate entrance leading to a comfortable waiting room. They then went to an attending room to see the physician and left by another door close to the dispensary. To the right of the front door was an accident room. On the upper floor there were two wards, one for men and one for women with each ward being capable of having three beds. There were three other rooms capable of becoming wards making a potential of 15 to 18 beds altogether. The walls of the wards were decorated with illuminated Scripture texts and there was a bookshelf with some volumes of cheerful Christian literature. There was also a moveable bath and hot and cold water in each room.

By 1890 the house had been renamed Victoria Home and in an effort to extend its usefulness any person of the poor artisan class or domestic servants were, in case of sickness, become a member of the dispensary on payment of five shillings and so at once be entitled to all the benefits of a well-appointed convalescent hospital.

In 1898 the fees were listed as:

A Child under the age of 14   1d per week
Single persons over the age of 14   2d per week
Family payments to include husband, wife   3d per week
and children under the age of 14
Domestic Servants   1s 6d per quarter
Midwifery cases   7s 6d each
No forfeits of fines of any description

In 1889 the dispensary had 2382 attendees with 34 subscribers with subs amounting to £41 8s 6d.

But not all was well with the management. Doctors working with the institution claimed the management was all by lay people who did not understand the problems and that they kept too much money in reserve instead of using it for services. They may have had a point as in 1879 the dispensary offered to donate £800 to the general fund to build the Princess Alice memorial hospital later increasing this to £1000 although nothing was actually donated in the end. Due to the ill feeling and the dispensary releasing some of the doctors they medical fraternity set up a rival institution called the Eastbourne Provident Medical Dispensary.

The original dispensary claimed this was done to enrich the doctors but this was denied and the doctors offered the members of the original dispensary to move over to them and 700 to 800 did and by 1898 they had a membership of 5338 with the population of Eastbourne being around 44,000. Despite this the Eastbourne Provident continued and became the Wellesley Trust.

Illustration 17: Chemist's advertisement

JOSEPH GIBBS,

Homœopathic & Dispensing Chemist,

TERMINUS ROAD, EASTBOURNE.

(Opposite the General Post Office.)

J. G. supplies Medicines in all forms—Pilules, Triturations, and Tinctures—and in all potencies. Since they are as far as possible, prepared by himself, they may be relied on as being fresh and effective.

GIBBS' FRAGRANT GLYCEROLE OR CALENDULA is one of the best applications for the skin in winter—fragrant, emollient and healing.

GIBBS' SUNBURN LOTION, the best application for the skin in summer.

PRESCRIPTIONS DISPENSED. The usual Toilet Articles, &c., accompanying a Chemist's business.

Eastbourne Health - Surgery

Surgery in early and mid-Victorian times was a brutal affair and was not much improved by the late Victorian times. Surgery was little short of butchery, painful and frequently fatal. Aside from the lack of knowledge, skill and training of the operators there were two vital components missing: anaesthesia and antisepsis. With the absence of the two essential components the unfortunate patients could expect considerable pain and almost inevitable post-operative infections.

In 1864 Dr Kidd, a surgeon from Guy's Hospital, London gave an insight into the relatively simple procedure for re-siting dislocated limbs before the use of chloroform. He described the use of pulleys and ropes in the procedure as being repulsive and mechanical. The pain the cripple experienced was great with the surgeon's assistant's foot in the scrotum (he did not identify whose scrotum the heel was in) and the students in relays pulling on ropes. During the efforts there would be horrible injury done to the torn capsule with the wretched patient crippled and writhing – still on the rack in torture. After such trauma the patient, hoping the procedure was successful, was expected to hop off the operating table and make their way to recovery. However, with the emergence of chloroform as an anaesthetic the manipulation of the bones avoided force, extensions and pulleys and by a little knack the head of the bone could be coaxed back into its place. The patient would feel little or no pain during the procedure with chloroform working a revelation is surgery. The problem was that because the patient undergoing the surgery felt no pain it emboldened the surgeons to take on longer and more complicated surgical procedures which actually raised the likelihood of post-operative infections such as gangrene and, as a result, an increased death rate.

The most common type of surgery that Eastbourne residents would have experienced was at the dental surgery where all operations were undertaken without anaesthetic until the emergence of nitrous oxide. Mr B L Mosely a dentist in Regent Street London in 1884 noted the daily experience of hospital and extensive private practice which demonstrated that unlike every other anaesthetic the nitrous oxide gas was innocuous and even pleasant while want of success or the least pain was simply impossible. In 1899 Mr Frederick Wells RDS offered painless dentistry in Eastbourne. A 10 year resident in the town and working out of the Cottage, Grove Road he did not profess to be the cheapest dentist but he guaranteed his work for five years and he offered painless extractions using nitrous oxide for five shillings.

By the end of the nineteenth century Louis Pasteur had identified "germs" as being the cause of infections and proposed that they could be killed. Joseph Lister was interested in the potential and, despite arguments to the contrary, introduced weak carbolic acid hand and surgical instrument washes as well as an air spray to kill off the "germs". Once the medical fraternity had understood that the antisepsis treatment was to prevent infection rather than cure it the principles were readily adopted.

In at least two areas the surgical procedures were becoming more acceptable and successful. But who was to deliver such services in a small town like Eastbourne with no hospital capable of performing such techniques? If anyone was to have an accident and break or dislocate a bone they would, initially, be taken to the relevant medical man's surgery. That would be the local 'general practitioner' who would try to mend the bone or relocate it.

If other surgery was required it might be left to people like George Gilbert. In 1884 the Independent Chapel in Heathfield fifteen miles north of Eastbourne, celebrated its 114th anniversary. It had been built in 1769 for George Gilbert, Apostle of Sussex. He was an ex-soldier who became a minister and preached in more than 40 parishes. At the time there was no regular medical practitioner, let alone hospital, in the area but George had kept a good supply of useful drugs and a case of instruments both of which he made use of for the relief of his poor neighbours.

So dentists, the odd bloke with a set of knives, barbers and those with some medical training could call themselves a surgeon and operate on any poor unfortunate needing attention. In 1866 the conductors of the Swedish railway were to be instructed in surgery so that they could assist in case of injury. An ambulance and medicine wagon was to accompany each train. Quite how dangerous Swedish trains were was not stated but it was strongly recommended that the proposals should be brought to the attention of English railway directors. Presumably the fireman could, between stoking the engine boilers, be required to perform the odd operation between stations. If you were at home rather than travelling you could perhaps refer to *Cassells Family Magazine* and read an article under the heading "Little Hints on Household Surgery". The first article was on how to apply a plaster and treat a cut. Possibly, as a build-up part work it would escalate advice to brain surgery.

To bring some order to the burgeoning profession the Earl de Grey proposed in 1870 establishing a Medical Board before which every person intending to practice medicine or surgery had to pass before being legally qualified. He noted there were 19 authorities in the UK empowered to grant diplomas but they differed in quality very much. He demanded that there should be one new and uniform examination which all medical practitioners should pass. Summing up the current situation he noted that quacks were allowed to do pretty much as they liked. When this was palming off ineffective medicines it might not be so serious but when they were proposing surgery then the outcomes could be more serious. The Medical Act came into force in 1886 and it caused a rush of what were described as idle young medical students to get on the medical register. Sadly it admitted that the vested rights of practitioners who were already registered with inferior and, in some cases, defective qualifications were preserved. The conclusion being that a multitude of the present generation would have to be put up with being killed in an irregular and unscientific manner.

So standards were being raised and two pupils of Eastbourne schools were celebrated as being successful in theory medical and surgical studies. In 1884 Mr Fourness Henry Simmons who matriculated from New College in 1880 passed the Edinburgh University Medical School examinations for the degree of Bachelor of Medicine and Master of Surgery gaining first class honours ad first medal as special prize for Operative Midwifery and Gynaecology. As he was passing out Mr Willie Lockwood who, for several years, had been a pupil at Clifton House in Eastbourne passed his first professional examinations for the degree of Bachelor of Medicine and Master in Surgery also in Edinburgh.

But all was not well in the world of surgery. The medical officer of health in Southwark stated that 526 persons "have come to as an untimely end as if they had been swept off the Earth by a platoon of musketry". If they had resided in Eastbourne they would have been in possession of life and fulfilling the duties that life demanded of them. In 1889 there was news of a disastrous episode of brain surgery reported in the newspapers. A patient at the Regent's Park Hospital in London had been told he would die in a few months at the latest if he did not have an operation. He had the operation and died four weeks later.

In 1899 the first van built for the London Anti Vivisection Society toured the country and paid a visit to Eastbourne for a week in September. Their main argument was that vivisection was a sin and claimed that doctors gained knowledge by torturing the lower creatures for the advantage of man. In their addresses to the town Dr Timothy Holman asserted that, in his opinion, the first object of hospitals was the instruction of students, the second object was the relief of suffering. Dr Burney Yeo stated that in various quarters surgical operations were constantly performed not for the advantage of the patient but solely for the pecuniary benefit of the operators. Dr Jackson, a lecturer in surgery to the Medical School in Sheffield denounced the reckless manner in which operations were performed in hospitals and it was to the recklessness that he attributed the frequent deaths.

In 1875 a Dr Dupre offered a different type of hygienic surgery which actually involved no bodily invasion at all. He treated the son of a worker at the Leaf Hall who was emaciated and had double posterior curvature of the spine, enormous abscesses and paralysis of the lower limbs as well as experiencing constant and severe pain. Using what he called hygienic surgery the doctor caused the abscesses to break down and discharge matter and through diet, bathing and calisthenics together with the use of non-poisonous medicines he cured the boy.

If non-invasive surgery worked it was claimed in 1898 that although the Leaf hospital was well adapted for providing the poor who desired to be treated homoeopathically there could be no such thing as homeopathic surgery. It was pointed out that in 1893 only three patients suffering from accidents, and those of a simple matter, had been admitted to the Leaf and their needs could have been amply provided for by the Princess Alice Memorial Hospital. There they could have been attended by their own medical men or by one of the medical officers on the staff.

In 1893 the Guardians of the Eastbourne union invited applications for the appointment of a medical officer to the workhouse. They would receive a salary of £120 a year with the usual extra fees (unspecified). All medicines except quinine and cod liver oil would have to be supplied at the cost of the officer elected. One might assume there would be a lot of prescriptions for cod liver oil. To ensure competence the applicants were required to be legally qualified medical practitioners under the existing laws relating to the practice of medicine and surgery in England and Wales and be able to supply diplomas, certificates or licences to practice with their applications.

So surgeons were becoming better educated and more skilled, anaesthetics took the pain out of surgery and aseptic techniques gave them a better chance of recovery. But in 1896 although there was some interest in Professor Rontgen's new discovery it was considered to be of little practical use in surgery. X rays had some work to do to become accepted.

Eastbourne Health – Surgical Aid Society

The Surgical Aid society was formed in1862 with a branch being formed, with the Right Honourable Marquis of Hartington as patron in Eastbourne in 1891. The society endeavoured to assist people who required appliances after attending hospital through illness or accident providing they were of a needy and deserving character. In 1899 it was noted that the cost of many appliances and artificial limbs would place them quite beyond the reach of numberless necessitous cases but for the merciful interposition of the society. In 1895 the Reverend Weeks had observed that there were Christians who were very fond of distributing tracts but the most effective way of carrying out the spirit of the Master and of rendering a real service was to give a loaf to a starving man and an appliance to an injured one.

And they certainly did give out appliances. In the year to September 1892 10,887 people, nationally had been helped with an average of 210 a week giving out 16,817 appliances which added up to 163,900 appliances distributed between children of a few weeks old and men and women of over ninety years of age since the society was formed. In Eastbourne in 1898 they reported that during the previous year 229 surgical appliances had been given to 188 people in Eastbourne when only 99 had been distributed the year before. In 1899 they listed giving out 13 abdominal belts, 5 sets of artificial teeth, 19 elastic web bandages, 13 pairs of spectacles, 18 trusses, 18 high cork and special boots, 2 leg irons and boots, 28 elastic stockings, 1 water pillow and 4 pairs of crutches.

But all this generosity and the fact that the town's population was increasing by 1500 to 1600 a year with most being working class meant that financing was an issue. In 1898 they had to go for financing to the parent society as subscriptions had fallen and were not covering the costs. At the start the following among the general public was low with the first annual general meeting only attracting nine people. It was regretted there were so few and that there were no women but it was put down to the inclement weather. There were appeals to the well-to-do to support the society through subscriptions which could be used to nominate deserving cases. The nominee for help would then attend a surgeon appointed by the society who would certify what appliances were necessary.

In 1892 the subscriptions to the society were 10/6d for one year and 5 guineas (£5 5s) for lifetime subscriptions. For this sum the subscriber was entitled to two recommendations for support per annum. Aid was only administered when letters nominating potential recipients were delivered by subscribers.

In 1912 the Surgical Aid Society became the Royal Surgical Aid society under King George V. In 1949 there were fears that the society would close after being nationalised but although some services were taken over by the new National Health Service the society still exists today.

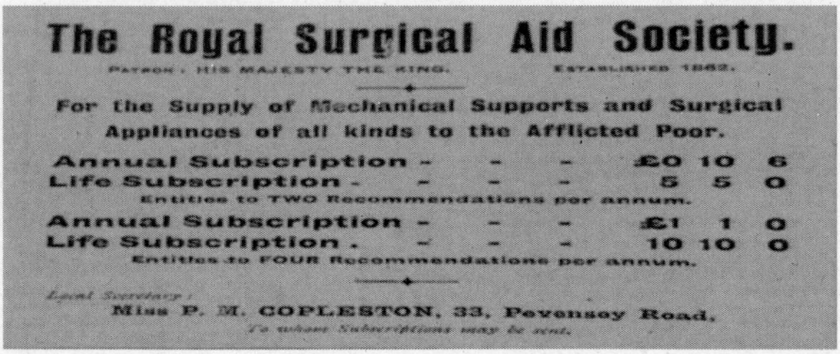

Illustration 18: Surgical Aid Society terms

Other Books in this series:

Everyday Life in Victorian Eastbourne

ISBN: 978 0 9926161 3 7

Everyday life in Between the Wars Eastbourne

ISBN: 978 0 9926161 4 4

Also from the same author:

A Spartan at Plataea

ISBN: 978 0 9926161 1 3

A description of what everyday life was like for a Spartan soldier in Classical period Greece

Partition

ISBN: 978: 0 9926161 2 0

A Supernatural thriller with a group based in Eastbourne trying to prevent the increase in technology destroying the partition between the living and the spirit world and hence the world.

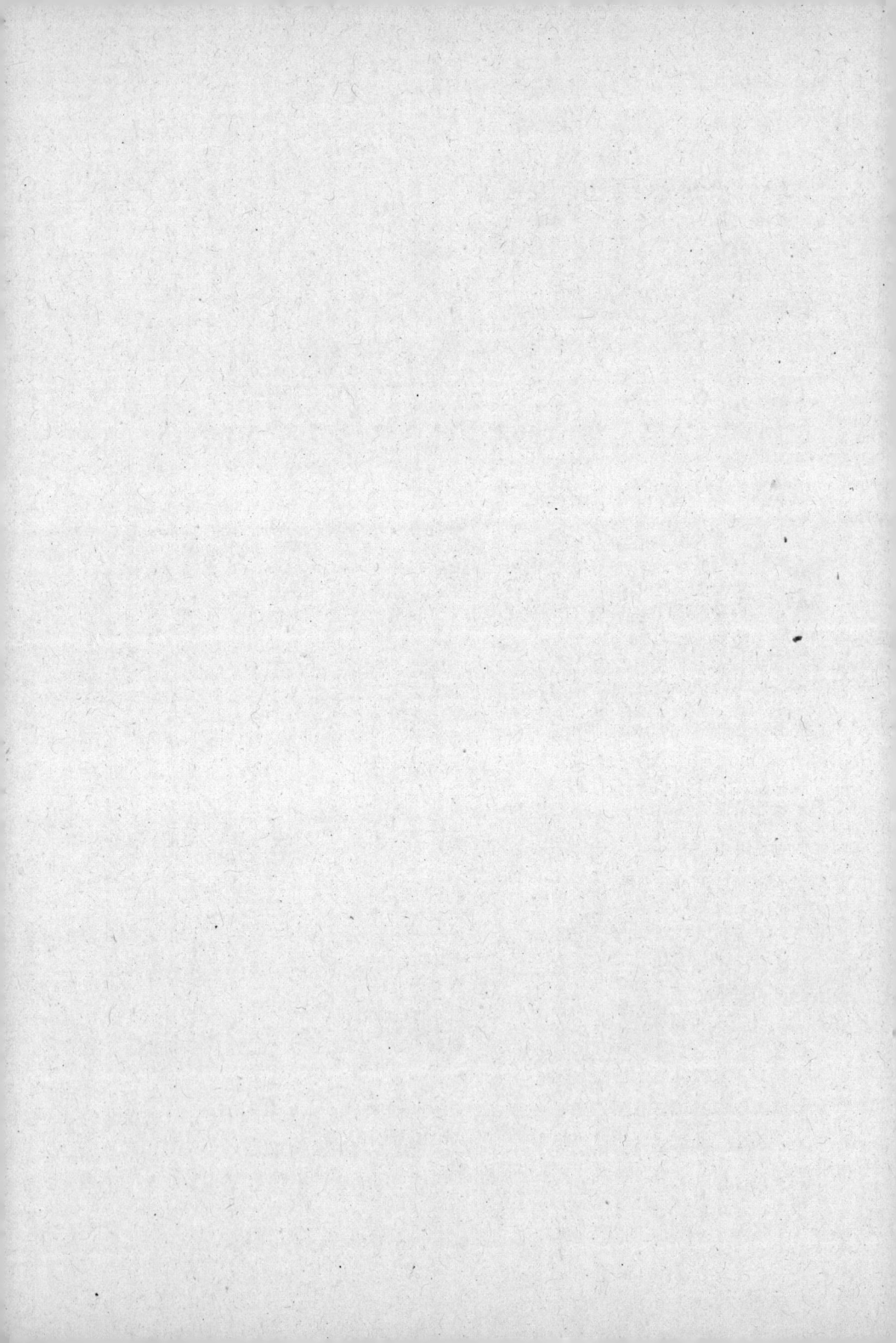